100 GREAT BRITS

James Muirden

summersdale

100 GREAT BRITS

Summersdale Publishers Ltd
46 West Street
Chichester
West Sussex
PO19 1RP
UK

www.summersdale.com

Printed and bound in Finland.

ISBN: 1-84024-611-1
ISBN 13: 978-1-84024-611-7

100 GREAT BRITS
A rhyming history from Bede to Beckham

James Muirden

This book is dedicated to
Great Brits everywhere

PREFACE

In 2002, the BBC conducted a viewers' poll to derive a list of the hundred 'greatest' Brits in order of popularity. I used this as a reference when starting work on this book, and I kept about half of them, having decided to exclude (with one or two exceptions) monarchs and career politicians, as well as well-known moderns who are likely to prove ephemeral. I did not, in any case, set out to compile a list of 'greatest' Brits, since enthusiasm had to drive my rhyming. I am afraid that a few short-listed worthies were excluded because I found them dull.

Being free to use my own definition of a 'Brit', I have had it both ways by including naturalised foreigners such as T. S. Eliot, and Brits by birth who have taken another nationality, such as Alistair Cooke.

Regarding titles, I have tried not to be too fussy. Knights and dames are so indicated. Peerages from baron to earl, whether inherited or bestowed, are simply indicated as, for example, 'Laurence Kerr, Lord Olivier' when the title takes the possessor's surname, but as, for example, 'William Richard Morris (Lord Nuffield)' when the title is linked to a place. Dukes, the highest rank of the peerage, are given their titles in full.

I would like to thank Merrily Harpur for her delightful illustrations. Jennifer Barclay's editorial eye has prompted improvements to several of the poems. As always, my wife Helen has been a tower of strength, helping me to choose suitable candidates and finding out more about the awkward ones.

James Muirden

BEDE

C. 672 – 26 MAY 735

The first historian of England

Not many people ever read
the venerable works of Bede,
which seems to me a crying shame.
The government must take the blame,
for Latin, sadly, has become
divorced from the curriculum;
no longer need they learn off pat
the verb *amo, amas, amat*.
But if they could, what fun to read
the venerable words of Bede!

In Tyne and Wear (its modern name)
Bede lived and died and earned his fame –
he went to Jarrow, it is stated,
when ten years old, and vegetated
(in other words, he put down roots).
His intellectual pursuits
within the cell he occupied
made him adored before he died –
they're all set out for you to read
in the surviving works of Bede!

A principal concern of his
was writing learned commentaries,
resolving points of Holy Writ
where statements didn't seem to fit.
He also helped to calculate
when Easter falls (a vital date),

pioneered musical notation,
deduced the date of the Creation,
foretold the lunar phase... Indeed,
all knowledge fascinated Bede!

In 731 appeared
the work for which he's most revered –
a five-part English History
from roughly 55 BC
(when Caesar came, and went away)
till what was then the present day.
His scholarship is still respected:
he judged his sources, and rejected
the dodgy ones that might mislead.
Such thoroughness began with Bede!

This saintly scholar was interred
at Durham; but a slip occurred
when his inscription was translated.
The words upon his coffin stated
his 'venerable bones' were there;
but thanks to lack of skill or care,
the word became conferred upon
the Man, and not his Skeleton.
And that is why we wrongly read
about the 'Venerable Bede'.

2.

ST BONIFACE (WINFRID)

C. 675 – 5 JUNE 754

A force for the spread of Christianity in Europe

Though born about the time of Bede,
and equally devout
in faith and prayer and thought and deed,
Winfrid was keener to succeed
in casting Light on those in need,
and sorting Pagans out!

A Benedictine monk, he yearned
to preach, convert and bless
in Europe, where (as he had learned)
by no means everyone had turned
to Jesus Christ; at last he earned
his Abbot's grudging 'Yes!'

Winfrid converted by the Book,
instilling faith through prayer –
except once, when he undertook
to fell Thor's sacred oak, which shook
the Pagans, for it didn't look
as if their god was there!

However, his success created
more paperwork, alas!
Pope Gregory was captivated
by how well he administrated,
and had our hero consecrated
as Bishop Boniface...

He thrived in his new-found vocation
until he reached its peak –
Primate of the conglomeration
that turned into the German nation!
But of his rise and culmination
there is no room to speak.

At last, in his declining years,
he gave up Crook and Mitre,
and set off with some volunteers
to preach once more; but it appears
he was attacked by men with spears
and died, Christ's willing fighter...

The Dutch and Germans, by the way,
revere him more than we.
He's still their patron saint today;
but in his homeland, sad to say,
this influential émigré
evokes a curt 'Who's he?'

3

ALFRED THE GREAT
C. 849 – 26 OCTOBER 899

Founder of the Anglo-Saxon nation

King Alfred made us who we are.
He checked the Danes, no less...
If he had not, we would say 'Ja'
instead of saying 'Yes'!

For years they'd run adventure trips,
arriving when it suited,
and leaving in their high-prowed ships
with all the stuff they'd looted.

Eventually the North and East
were seriously depressed.
Assaults on Wessex now increased
(that was the South and West.)

King Alfred's family ruled here.
If Danish troops broke through,
the island's hopes would disappear,
and that would never do!

His men, alas, were put to flight
when Guthrum's troops attacked
at Chippenham, around Twelfth Night
(a most unseasonal act).

A cottager gave him a bed...
When told to watch the cakes,
they slipped his mind (or so it's said).
He made no more mistakes.

With all the manpower he could get,
he routed Guthrum's force
at Edington, in Somerset –
this altered Britain's course![1]

The Danes agreed that they'd retreat,
and future raids were banned.
'Danelaw' was east of Watling Street;[2]
the rest was Angle-Land!

---

1   The Battle of Edington, Easter 878
2   Watling Street followed part of the course of the A5.

Fights followed through succeeding reigns,
despite the pact they'd signed,
and What To Do About The Danes
was constantly in mind

until his grandson, Athelstan,
cleared most of them away,
fulfilling Alfred's master plan
to rule the land one day![3]

That's not the only reason, though,
he's held in such esteem.
The 'burghs' or boroughs that we know
began with Alfred's scheme

to organise the land's defence,
manned by a standing force.
Which needed Laws and Documents,
and Bureaucrats, of course!

And also, this accomplished king
translated Bede (q.v.)
into Old English – just the thing
to pass an hour or three...

When he had given all he'd got,
his corpse was laid in state.
His bones are lost, his name is not –
he's earned the title 'Great'.

---

3   Athelstan (r. 927–939) was effectively the first King of England.

ST THOMAS BECKET
21 DECEMBER 1118 – 29 DECEMBER 1170

An uncompromising Archbishop of Canterbury

King Henry II
was wrong to have reckoned
that Thomas, his off-duty friend,
wouldn't change in the least
when made England's Top Priest –
that's when his allegiance would end!

Henry made the mistake
of trying to take
the laws of the Church for his own.
The bishops should not
use the powers they'd got
to make judgments that bypassed the Throne!

But the Crook and the Mitre
made Thomas a fighter.
For God (and not King) he now stood...
So Henry, checkmated,
is claimed to have stated:
'I'd get rid of this guy, if I could!'

Four knights overheard,
and having conferred,
they set out, unknown to the king
(or so it is thought),
and cut Thomas off short.
The news of this terrible thing
caused Henry regret,

for his hopes had been set
on making a pact in the end.
Barefooted, he crept
to the relics they'd kept
of his rapidly-canonised friend.[1]

In this struggle we see,
as with More (q.v.),
that when Might and Conviction dispute,
though the stronger may slay,
at the end of the day
it's the loser we hold in repute!

---

1   The Pope declared Becket a saint in 1173 – a record for speed. King
Henry made his penance on 12 July 1174.

5.

KING ARTHUR

RE-BORN C. 1138, STILL GOING STRONG

A legendary Briton c.500

Did Arthur and his knights exist,
as vested interests insist?
With stone-snatched sword in mailed fist,
did he triumphantly resist
that Anglo-Saxon lot?
Did Guinevere become his Queen?
Did gallants joust upon the green
presenting a resplendent scene
at courtly Camelot?

If so, his re-birth had to wait
until 1138.
Six hundred years he'd lain in state
(though nobody can now locate
our hero's hallowed spot).
Geoffrey of Monmouth is the key
to our 'King Arthur' industry,
for in his British History[1]
he gives the biggest spot

to Arthur, and of course his knights,
who regularly win their fights
against the Saxons, which unites
the Brits. He has a shot
at conquering all Europe too –

---

1   *Historia Regnum Britanniae, c.*1138

the sort of thing a king should do;
but while he is away, guess who
has hatched a devilish plot?

His nephew Mordred has rebelled!
Queen Guinevere is being held —
the insurrection must be quelled!
They fight at Camlan – Arthur's felled!
The faithful men he's got
take him to Avalon. This done,
Queen Guinevere becomes a nun,
and soon the country's overrun.
(I've shortened it somewhat.)

Was all this based on fact? Maybe.
But then Sir Thomas Malory[2]
gave Geoffrey's homespun history
a truly epic quality...
He makes Sir Lancelot
elope to Gaul with Guinevere,
and many other knights appear,
including bold Sir Bedevere,
to bolster up the plot!

Le Morte d'Arthur, his famous fable,[3]
extols the Roundness of the Table –
a knightly accolade or label
bestowed on the supremely able
(an entertaining lot).
They even set off on the trail
to find the Cup, or Holy Grail;
it is an entertaining tale,
but history it's not!

---

2   Thomas Malory *c.*1407–1471
3   Published by William Caxton (q.v.), 1485

6

ROBERT THE BRUCE
11 JULY 1274 – 7 JUNE 1329

Who made Scotland into a recognised kingdom

'Scots Wha Hae' (revised version)

Scots wha hae defied the foe,
I'm your monarch, as you know!
Back me up, and we shall go
on to Victory!

England's Edward No. 1
has all Scotland on the run!
Nothing further can be done –
hang on patiently!

What's the point of being king?
I'm not ruling anything!
How about another fling?
Routed! Got to flee![1]

In the Hebrides I sit.
Watch that Spider for a bit.
Edward's dying? This is it!
I scent Victory!

---

1   Battle of Methven, 19 June 1306

A RHYMING HISTORY

Raise your sporrans! England's through!
This King Edward No. 2
simply hasn't got a clue!
Fight alongside me!

Tide of fortune starts to turn...
Sort them out at Bannockburn...[2]
Wave goodbye – they won't return!
Edward No. 3

sees that battling's no use,
and signs an everlasting truce.
Gives yours truly, Robert Bruce,
Scotland's sovereignty!

---

2   23–24 June 1314

7.

GEOFFREY CHAUCER

C. 1343 – 25 OCTOBER 1400

'The Father of English Literature'

'When that Aprilis, with his showers swoot,
the drought of March hath piercèd to the root...'[1]
with such a Spring did Chaucer's genius bless
our literary scene with Englishness!
Before his birth, it was receivèd truth
(since our vernacular was so uncouth),
that French, not Middle English, was the tongue
in which emotion must be rhymed or sung.
This is what all the world considered then,
till in the native font he dipped his Pen.

Though William Langland, also of that time,[2]
wrote Middle English too, it didn't rhyme.
He used an earlier style, where words rebounded
within each line, as consonants were sounded –
he might have written, had he lived today,
'the mournful music of the motorway'
(three words begin with 'm' – a demonstration
of what the experts call 'alliteration').
The French had rhymed the final word for ages,
so Chaucer took a leaf out of their pages!

---

1   These are the first two lines of the Prologue to the *Canterbury Tales*.
2   Langland (*c.*1330–*c.*1386) wrote *Piers Plowman*.

About his youthful years, much is obscure.
We know the Father of our Literature
was born into a family of means;
he served a Lady when he reached his teens,
and once he'd grown to manhood, it is thought,
he moved within the orbit of the Court.
Edward III, in 1374,
gave him a dole of wine for evermore
(a gallon every day), which does suggest
that by our poet's Pen he was impressed.

He started writing seriously, it's thought,
when made comptroller (boss) of London's port;
a job that left sufficient hours free
for him to have a go at poetry.
One piece that he is still remembered for –
a lovers' tale from the Trojan War,
Troilus and Cressida, was used much later
by Shakespeare (q.v.), our Regurgitator.
But what made Geoffrey Chaucer truly Great
was what he did in 1388...

St Thomas Becket (q.v.) was interred
at Canterbury (where his death occurred),
and pilgrims trudged there, sharing the belief
that saints could intercede and bring relief;
they'd fast-track Purgatory, if your request
was to their relics properly addressed!
A pilgrimage would bring all sorts together
to share discomfort, danger, and the weather;
and Chaucer's trek, it seems, inspired the setting
for all the different Tales he was begetting...

The Canterbury Tales we have today
are but a part (a fifth, I've heard some say)
of the projected blockbuster he'd planned.
He had all the material to hand;
a Technicolor eye, the widest screen,
the vastest cast that Literature had seen,
or would see, till the Avon Bard began
to write of Kings and of the Common Man!
In Poets' Corner you will find his tomb –
he lay there first, which gave him lots of room.[3]

---

3   In Westminster Abbey

8.

OWAIN GLYNDŴR

C. 1359 – C. 1416

Who tried to give Wales a recognised monarchy

I'm Owain Glyndŵr...
My name rhymes with 'Power',
and that's what this story's about.
My attempt to free Wales
admittedly fails;
but I try hard – of that there's no doubt!

Long before I was born,
we had been quite a thorn
in the side of King Edward I.
He built castles to prove
that the slightest false move
meant the likes of us coming off worst!

I was duly conceived,
and at long last received
the estates that my family held.
And with Henry IV
campaigning up north,
I jumped at the chance, and rebelled!

Support wasn't lacking
thanks to powerful backing
from Hotspur, Northumberland's son;
whose family wished
to see Henry's hopes dished,
and a new line of monarchs begun!

In 1403
the plan was for me
to join him at Shrewsbury, where
our armies would meet,
attack, and defeat
Prince Hal, aged 16, Henry's heir!

But a fight that I fought
hadn't gone as it ought,
and I didn't arrive when I should.
Perhaps I was lucky,
for Hotspur, though plucky,
was beaten – so that was no good!

But I never despaired.
To the Welsh, I declared:
'The English will give up and leave
if we take to the hills
and develop our skills
as guerrillas!' It's hard to believe

but Harlech soon fell,
Aberystwyth as well;
which of course was an excellent sign!
But our hopes began fading
when Prince Hal came raiding.
We fought on till 1409

when both castles were lost
at great personal cost,
for my wife and my children were seized.
In 1413,
with Hal crowned, he was keen[1]
to forgive me. I wasn't too pleased

---

1   As Henry V

at the thought of kowtowing,
so I hid away, vowing
that I'd die in the hills with my men.
But if, as I hear,
a day in the year
may be *mine*, then I'll turn up again![2]

WILLIAM CAXTON

C₀ 1422 - C₀ 1491

The first English printer

A merchant in Bruges, then in Burgundy's grip,
he had started translating (for fun)
a book about Troy; and the Duchess let slip
that she'd like him to order her one...

He knew that her trend-setting choice would excite
a demand that outstripped the supply.
Then he heard of a clever device that could *write*
(at least, *print*) – so he gave it a try!

A RHYMING HISTORY

The type he employed was intended to look
like the shapes that the clerics were using;
for the public would not be impressed by the book
if the text looked too strange and confusing!

So the first book in English was printed at Bruges
(for the Duchess was English, in fact).
Caxton saw that the method's potential was huge –
in time all the scribes would be scrapped!

Troy was probably printed in '74,[1]
and the venture was such a success
(it's thought that he ran off five hundred or more)
that he then did a book about chess.[2]

He came back to London the following year,
set up his own press, and began
(well into his fifties) a second career
in the book trade. This talented man

translated and edited, printed and bound
a hundred new titles or so!
But when Richard III was so doubtfully crowned,
Caxton's stock fell exceedingly low

since the Duchess, his patron, was most disapproving
of the King who'd allegedly slain
both the Princes (her kin); but with Richard's removing,
his press started pressing again!

---

1   *Recuyell of the Historyes of Troye* (1474)
2   *The Game and Playe of the Chesse* (1475)

Caxton's editing skills had a greater effect
than you may have supposed at first sight,
for he started defining what forms were *correct*
in the English that people would write.

Chaucer's *Tales* and Malory's *Arthur* (q.v.)
both sold well – but the Bible? No way!
To translate the Good Book, as you'll very soon see,
was considered unlikely to pay![3]

---

3   See the entry for William Tyndale.

10.

SIR THOMAS MORE
7 FEBRUARY 1478 – 6 JULY 1535

Who would not compromise his faith

The Chancellor of England, Thomas More,
never gave way upon a point of law.
A staff of oak may break, but will not bend;
the gale swayed him not, so in the end
he had to be demolished with an axe.
Before then, though, he ran on oiled tracks –
lawyer, then barrister, then an administrator
in London's courts; and not all that much later,
a personal adviser to the King
(Henry VIII), so things were flourishing!

He led a life beyond the 9–5...
His most important writings to survive
are, first, *Utopia*, about a land
where all's in common. Private wealth is banned;
house, clothes and work are ordered by the State;
they work six hours, and go to bed at eight.
He gets a lower rating for the second
(*Richard III*); it's generally reckoned
that More set out to blacken Richard's name
to help the Tudors' rather shaky claim
when he was overthrown. Shakespeare (q.v.)
immortalised Richard's anatomy![1]

---

[1]   As 'crookback Richard'

Henry VIII was anxious for a son.
However, Catherine (Wife No. 1)
did not produce the princeling he desired.
So Anne Boleyn, a lady he admired,
was pencilled in to be Wife No. 2.
Divorce was Out; the only thing to do
was to call Catherine's marriage null and void.
Henry became increasingly annoyed
when Wolsey, though his Chancellor of State,
failed to make the Pope co-operate,
so More stepped into Wolsey's shoes instead.
The marriage with Boleyn then went ahead
without the Pope's sought-after dispensation,
but More did not attend her coronation.
To him, the Pope was God's own appointee –
what God refused to sanction, must not be!
King Henry didn't share this point of view –
the Pope ruled Rome, but not the English too.
The crisis came when More was given a quill
and told to sign approval of a Bill
that made the Church subservient to the Crown.
He held his hand, and so the axe came down.
I'm sorry that this poem's short on wit,
but saintly people hamper me a bit.[2]

---

2   Thomas More was canonised in 1935, exactly 400 years after his
death. He is the patron saint of lawyers and statesmen.

WILLIAM TYNDALE

C. 1490 – 6 OCTOBER 1536

Who printed the New Testament in English, and paid for it

It seemed to Tyndale quite absurd
that simple people only heard
a Latin text (which priests preferred).
And so he privately averred,
regardless of the risks incurred,
that he would translate every word
Lord Jesus had to say!

He knew, before he tackled it,
that Church decree did not permit
such monkeying with Holy Writ.
Could *comprehension* benefit?
A Bishop nearly had a fit![1]
But Tyndale on the bullet bit,
and started anyway...

England was not the place to be.
The safest place was Germany,
where parts were relatively free
of Roman-based authority,
since Martin Luther made them see
that simple Faith should turn the key –
and not the way you pray!

---

1   Cuthbert Tunstall (1474–1559), Bishop of London, who turned
     William out of his palace.

So, in disguise, away he slipped
with the explosive manuscript.
Cologne had somebody equipped
to print it, but the place was gripped
by Popery, so off he nipped
to Worms. The printed books were shipped[2]
to shops in the UK

(forgive me the anachronism),
inspiring a paroxysm
of virulent antagonism...
This odious vernacularism
proved him a tool of Lutheranism;
for such bare-faced hereticism
he must be made to pay!

This level of displeasure meant
a long stay on the Continent;
ten years in total Tyndale spent
in studious concealment
(nobody's certain where he went),
translating the Old Testament –
from Hebrew, by the way!

Eventually, he was caught
(a 'friend' betrayed him, it is thought),
when he was still a few Books short.
He was imprisoned in a fort
near Brussels, went before a court,
a charge of heresy was brought,
and Tyndale blazed away...

---

2   Worms was a safer city in which to be Protestant.

But now King Henry thought he'd need
a Bible everyone could read
(its accuracy guaranteed);
he told his clerics to proceed,
and do it with the utmost speed.
The working-party all agreed
that Tyndale's was OK![3]

So thanks to that, his legacy
survives in our phraseology.
'Salt of the earth', 'the powers that be',
'let there be light'... he's possibly
done more for our vocabulary
than even Shakespeare did (q.v.).
Let's honour him today!

---

3   The Great Bible, published in 1539, was the forerunner of the
defining King James Bible of 1611.

12

SIR FRANCIS DRAKE

C. 1540 – 27 JANUARY 1596

Who circumnavigated the world, and beat the Spanish

Here's to Old England and Admiral Drake,
robbing the Spanish for fun!
Loading his vessels with all he could take –
silver and gold by the ton!
Bess was impressed by the profit he made,
and sent off the *Golden Hind*
on a carefully-planned South American raid
to pinch what the Spanish had mined.
Though a trader in slaves he had certainly been,
and a pirate he later became,
he atoned for it when the Armada was seen,
with the words: 'I'll just finish this game!'

He sailed round the Horn, a remarkable feat,
collecting the treasure he sought
as he went up the coast, having lost all his fleet.
Then he crossed the Pacific, and bought
upmarket delights such as spice, with the gold
that the Spaniards had kindly provided,
reaching Plymouth with twice England's wealth in the hold,
which Drake and his monarch divided!
Though a trader in slaves he had certainly been,
and a pirate he later became,
he atoned for it when the Armada was seen,
with the words: 'I'll just finish this game!'

A RHYMING HISTORY

England singed, as we put it, the Spanish King's beard
(he had tried to win Bess and her realm)
when in front of their fleet in Cadiz we appeared,
and wrecked it, with Drake at the helm!
And when the Armada reached Calais at last,
thanks to fire-ships puffed by the breeze,
the Spanish were scattered, the danger was past,
and Bess was the Queen of the Seas!
Though a trader in slaves he had certainly been,
and a pirate he later became,
he atoned for it when the Armada was seen,
with the words: 'I'll just finish this game!'

He could have retired, and lived off his treasure –
but that was too boring for Drake!
He wasn't a man who was happy with leisure;
he liked hazard for hazard's own sake.
He enjoyed South American raiding the most,
where he died – not by cannon or shot,
but from dysentery, anchored off Panama's coast.
And that, as we say, was his lot!
So let's wipe the slate clean of the errors he made,
and give thanks for this leader of men.
For he sounded his Drum when we needed his aid;
and he'll hear if we beat it again!

13.

JOHN NAPIER
(LAIRD OF MERCHISTON)

C. 1550 – 4 APRIL 1617

Who facilitated mathematical calculation,
especially by the use of logarithms

John Napier was truly Great
to those who had to calculate
before the days of the Machine.
The hardest sum you've ever seen,
the deepest Root, the highest Power,
which might have taken half an hour
of tedious pencil-blunting slog,
was just like falling off a log!
Yes, *logarithms* were the key
to scientific numeracy
for 350 years,
until the silicon chip appears.

Can I explain in verse? I'll try!
Suppose we wish to multiply
100 x 1000, say,
using the logarithmic way...
100 is 10^2, and so
its log is 2; we also know
1000 is 10^3, i.e.
its logarithm must be 3.
Now, 3 and 2 add up to 5;
so by addition we arrive
at 10^5, which, you will find

(if you're of an enquiring mind)
is what you ought to hope to get
when doing the little sum I set.[1]
So logarithmic calculation
involves less mental perspiration:
to get two numbers multiplied
you *add* their logs; or to divide,
you *take* one of their logs away,
which basically is child's play.
Well, that's the best that I can do
to rhyme John Napier's method. Phew!

His *Rods* or *Bones* I'll also mention
(you may have heard of this invention).
This second calculating trick
required lengths of bone or stick
inscribed with numbers, side by side;
once more, this method *multiplied*
by adding up! What else? Let's see...
He studied agro-chemistry,
and so it's not at all surprising
he was a whizz at fertilising –
nobody then had ever seen
green fields of a greener green!
He also had a good idea
for making Spaniards disappear:
shine sunlight on their naval force
(choosing a cloudless day, of course)
and by its concentrated heat
burn up and sink King Philip's fleet!

---

1   That is, 100,000.

As well as setting fire to ships,
he worked on the Apocalypse,
and did a complex calculation
(based on the Book of Revelation)
that gave him 1688
as one potential Final Date.[2]
For once, I'm very glad to say,
his mathematics went astray!

---

2   Napier was a practising Protestant, and it is interesting that 1688
was the year of the 'Glorious Revolution', when the monarchy was
established as Protestant for all time.

SIR WALTER RALEIGH
C. 1554 – 29 OCTOBER 1618

A colourful adventurer

'Farewell to the Court' (revised version)

'Like truthless dreams, so are my joys expired,
and past return are all my dandled days...'
My trip to South America backfired –
I'm in the Tower, in my final phase!

Oh, when the Virgin Queen of me approved,
there wasn't anything I couldn't do.
How many chests of gold have I removed
from Spanish treasure vessels? Quite a few!

And that proud year of 1584!
With what great hopes I crossed the Pond for her,
and set foot on that far Atlantic shore
to found a colony – *Virginia*!

But when Spain's looters threatened to invade,
she wouldn't even let me put to sea!
Although I built a ship for her (and paid),
the glory went to Francis Drake (q.v.)!

Then things went really pear-shaped. Three years later,
Bess Throgmorton (her maid) and I were plighted.
The Queen was furious, called me a traitor,
and in a cell yours truly was benighted.

She let me out, but things weren't quite the same.
And then she died, and King James came to power.
On bogus charges (I was not to blame)
I spent no less than *twelve years* in the Tower!

I wrote a History of Ancient Greece
(now out of print), which occupied my mind.
Then some kind friend arranged for my release
to go to Venezuela, there to find

the gold of El Dorado! Off I went.
By this time Spain was friendlier with us.
But my men sacked a Spanish settlement,
So their ambassador was furious.

My son was killed during this foolish action,
and I returned bereaved and in disgrace.
A further reason for dissatisfaction
was that I never found the wretched place!

The Spanish want my head as compensation,
so here I am again, locked in my cell.
It's not a very happy situation,
considering things started off so well.

The axe-man says that I can have a look
and feel the blade before he lets it fall.
It's kind of you to put me in your book –
right now I don't feel very Great at all.

15.

FRANCIS BACON
(LORD ST ALBAN)

22 JANUARY 1561 – 9 APRIL 1626

Who advocated the 'scientific method'

Unless I'm very much mistaken,
if you refer to Francis Bacon,
someone will say: 'Oh, didn't he
really write Shakespeare's plays?' (q.v.)
However, Bacon would have said
such claims turn Reason on its head,
for they start with the *supposition*
that somebody in Will's position

(a merchant's son) could not acquire
the skill and learning he'd require;
and anyone convinced of this
would flesh out their hypothesis
by seeking facts to back their case!
But Bacon earns a noble place
among the Greats we have produced,
by saying truth can't be deduced
from 'laws' that might be altered later.
Science requires first-class data
based on painstaking measurements
or on controlled experiments;
from these we may *derive* the laws
that are the underlying cause!
His influence has been terrific
on everything that's scientific.

He held high public office, which
would normally have made him rich;
but King James kept a costly court,
which meant the Treasury was short,
and so official employees
would boost their meagre pay with fees
from those who came to plead or sue.
This was a dangerous thing to do,
and Bacon was arraigned and tried
for taking money on the side
(although we trust he wasn't swayed
by how much litigants had paid).
A few days in the Tower, and then,
free but disgraced, he whittled his pen,
bought lots of paper, and began
reflecting on the role of Man;
for better, and indeed for worse,
in this perplexing Universe.

A RHYMING HISTORY

Novum Organum was the start
(in the event, the only part)
of one great work to make the case
for strengthening our knowledge base;[1]
and here he offers some examples
of what you can deduce from samples...
For instance, every swan in sight
may be a similar shade of white;
but even though you never find
a colour of a different kind,
you cannot, on this basis, state
'All swans are white'. But if you wait
until a black swan comes in view,
then it is manifestly true
that not all swans are white; and so
what's *not* is easier to know!

Bacon's investigative bent
inspired an experiment
to see if meat would keep by freezing.
He tested the idea by seizing
(when he was going on his way
near Hampstead Heath one wintry day)
a chicken, which he duly filled
with snow (it had, of course, been killed).
This was, with hindsight, rather silly,
because he got extremely chilly,
his lungs were blocked, he couldn't speak,
and passed away within a week.
So do reflect on what he did
next time you lift the freezer lid.

---

1   *Novum Organum*, the 'New System', was published in Latin in 1620,
     just before his downfall. He wrote many other works, including an
     unfinished romance in English called *New Atlantis*.

16.

WILLIAM SHAKESPEARE

C. 23 APRIL 1564 – 23 APRIL 1616

Our greatest playwright and sonneteer

Shall I compare you to a summer's day?
What sun exceeds its season without setting?
What protean spring engendered play on play
(whose plots were rarely of your own begetting)?
Whose voice was it, that only you could hear?
What quill divine guided your human hand?
How can your words speak to the present ear
in sounds sublime, that we still understand?

Had we but half the harvest of his mind,
we should esteem our William no less well;
and that is all we could expect to find,
but for the pains of Heminge and Condell.
They printed all his plays, and saved *Macbeth*
(and umpteen others too) from dusty death![1]

---

1   John Heminge and Henry Condell collected up his 18 unpublished
       plays, and printed all his works (apart from *Pericles*) in the First Folio
       of 1623.

17.

THOMAS HOBBES

5 APRIL 1588 – 4 DECEMBER 1679

Who advocated autocratic government

Hobbes and Locke disagree
(as you'll presently see)
on how government ought to be run.
The latter professed
that the *masses* know best;
whereas Hobbes gave the power to *One*.[1]

In his view, we are not
a congenial lot;
in fact we are Beasts, nothing more.
Since Nature's a fight,
it's our natural right
to attack and defend, tooth and claw!

Thus, each person will strive
to survive (if not thrive);
life is nasty and brutish and short.
Hobbes does not, it is clear,
find much evidence here
for love of the God-given sort!

If the Nation's to cope,
there is only one hope –
to abandon our selfish desire,
and agree from now on
that autonomy's gone.
So a Ruler is what we require.

---

1   His theory of government is set out in *Leviathan*, 1651.

This Ruler's ambition
will improve our condition –
or so our reformer maintains...
If the State becomes greater,
then sooner or later
we'll all share the material gains!

But what, you may say,
if he's carried away,
and authority goes to his head?
Hobbes would answer: 'So what?
Despotic or not,
rebelling means chaos instead.'

It is certainly true
that the Hobbesian view
is at odds with beliefs we hold dear.
But are we so free
democratically?
And is it, in any case, clear

that we make the best choice
through a popular voice?
Are our leaders the best we can get?
Perhaps we should just
take a Ruler on trust –
though I can't see it happening yet!

18.

OLIVER CROMWELL
25 APRIL 1599 – 3 SEPTEMBER 1658

Who refused the Crown

Of all my splendid Brits, his claim to fame
is still the subject of opposing views.
A tyrant, or a leader with one aim –
the Best for Britain? Time for you to choose!

He was an MP, liked the countryside,
knew God was with him, had no large ambition.
But Charles I, whom Parliament defied,
dissolved the House, which altered the position.

Who ran the country, King or Parliament?
The crisis came in 1642,
and Oliver, who raised a regiment,
opposed the King, as he was bound to do!

His military prowess helped them win.
King Charles was safely under house arrest,
and Government by People could begin!
Though Cromwell was an MP like the rest,

he was the English Army's acting head.
When Charles refused to change the constitution,
Cromwell gave up, thought Charles was better dead,
and signed the warrant for his execution.

After the King's beheading, four years passed.
The 'Commonwealth' was hampered by division
within the ruling Council. Then, at last,
they came to an executive decision...

Cromwell was dubbed Protector of the Realm.
From 1653 until he died,
our hero steered unchallenged at the helm.
In fact he did so well, they even tried

to crown him as King Oliver I.
But Cromwell turned his back upon the throne.
Their policy could not now be reversed;
from now on, they must run the show alone.

But when he died and left an empty place,
the call for Charles II would begin.
Soon, Cromwell's corpse was dug up in disgrace.
The Merry Monarch reigned – so did Nell Gwynn...

19.

JOHN LOCKE

29 AUGUST 1632 – 28 OCTOBER 1704

A revolutionary philosopher

I've tried to take stock
of the greatness of Locke
(for great he undoubtedly was).
But between you and me,
philosophically,
he is giving me trouble, because

his writing's so dense!
Still, its overall sense
gave his readers a hell of a jolt.
He said nations could fight
a king's divine right
(if they had to) by open revolt!

But this only applies
if the ruler denies
the rights of each man and his neighbour,
which are earned (in Locke's view)
from the work that they do,
since it's on the *investment of labour*

that a country is founded.
Based on this, he propounded
his theory of government thus:
If you're ruled by command,
you can justly demand:
'Hand over the power to us!'

When Locke did his writing
the times were exciting,
for matters had come to a head.
The country sacked James
for his Catholic aims,
and brought in a new king instead

(i.e. William III),
a revolt that occurred
without blood being shed, which reflected
Locke's theory of choice –
if the general voice
wanted change, then change must be effected!

Would his ghost be amused
at the way he's been used
to defend revolution abroad?
France's popular coup –
the Americans too
when they cut the umbilical cord?

Something else that he taught
concerned *freedom of thought*
(a novelty then, by the way).
He wrote that all creeds
should respect others' needs –
not exactly the feeling today!

20.

SIR CHRISTOPHER WREN

20 OCTOBER 1632 – 25 FEBRUARY 1723

Who designed St Paul's, and many other things

Sir Christopher Wren often dined with some men,
and wide-ranging discussion there'd be,
from the distance of stars (still a mystery then)
to the number of legs on a flea!

There was change in the air; people thought that perhaps
we could find out a lot if we tried.
God couldn't go on keeping facts under wraps
if the brains he'd supplied were applied!

Wren's head was stuffed full of creative ideas,
from machines that sowed seeds in a row,
to devices that wrote, or that helped engineers
to pump water. He then had a go

at transfusing the blood from one dog to its friend,
and tried to improve navigation;
he studied how muscles make human joints bend,
and methods of fortification

and how to grind lenses, and hives that allowed
the bees to be seen through their walls.
A British da Vinci of whom to be proud,
long before he embarked on St Paul's!

Until he was 30 we don't hear a mention
of buildings he may have designed;
but his wide-ranging gifts came to people's attention,
so it isn't surprising to find

that he sat on a body set up by the Crown,
to consider the current position
of the old St Paul's church. To patch up or pull down,
in view of its parlous condition?

They discussed for some years, but couldn't agree.
Then the Fire of London broke out,
and once the smoke cleared it was easy to see
there was nothing to argue about.

He was 36 when he took charge of the plan,
and five sovereigns sat on the throne
(Kings Charles, James and William, Queens Mary and Anne),
till he watched his son fix the last stone

in the top of the dome, on which Wren had insisted,
although most people wanted a spire.[1]
Domes weren't for the Brits! No tradition existed,
yet this would be wider and higher

than anyone else had achieved until then
(apart from St Peter's in Rome).
They didn't intimidate Christopher Wren –
he was utterly set on his dome!

But that was just one of the tasks he fulfilled.
In all, 53 churches were wrecked;
their replacements he had to design and rebuild.
Oh yes, and he had to direct

the re-planning of London, which he would have based
around avenues long, wide and splendid.
But this meant that the city must first be laid waste
far beyond where the Fire had ended!

---

1   The first stone of the cathedral was laid on 21 June 1675, and it was
     finished in 1711, when Wren was 78.

A RHYMING HISTORY

There was no chance at all that his plan would succeed,
but his masterpiece stands on its hill;
and though concrete and glass its dimensions exceed,
Wren's dome uplifts Londoners still.

21.

SAMUEL PEPYS
23 FEBRUARY 1633 – 26 MAY 1703

A diarist of exciting times, 1660–1669

His last entry, 31 May 1669

...then to the 'World's End', merry, late returning.
And this, I fear, is all that I can write.
When I take up my pen, my eyes start burning;
to carry on, could jeopardise my sight.
So, come what may, I have made up my mind.
Henceforth, I'll have assistants do my writing;
no sins or indiscretions will you find,
which means it will be fairly unexciting!

Should I be told some merry anecdote,
I may employ the margin of my book
to make a crabbed and blotted short-hand note
whereon a puzzled eye may safely look.
But now, as on my corpse, it seems to me,
I close the cover of my Diary...

His elevation

His father, being well-connected,
pulled strings, and Samuel was selected
to work for Edward Montagu,
an advantageous thing to do,
for Montagu was made a Lord
when Charles II was restored.
His Diary's first year would mark
his elevation from a clerk
with scarce enough to light a fire
to everything he could desire –
a Whitehall post, attractive pay
(it worked out at £1 a day!)

His Diary

The famous Diary begins
some years after John Evelyn's,
and lasts for a decade or so;
Evelyn kept his on the go
for 65 years in the end –
a whole lot longer than his friend![1]
But still, the record Evelyn keeps
is much less fun than that of Pepys.
Knowing it could be dynamite,
he used a code in which to write

---

[1]   John Evelyn (1620–1706) kept his diary from 1641 until 1706.

(the entries all reflect his mood,
and some of them are rather rude).
Since 1660's opening day
he kept a record, come what may,
of great events, and small ones too –
we get a panoramic view
of high and low society.
Through his bewildered eyes, we see
plague-ravaged corpses heaped in carts;
the evening when the Fire starts;
amorous thoughts and conquests made...
He keeps it up for a decade,
then suddenly the entries end.
I've sonnetised the lines he penned
saying he's come to the decision
that diaries are bad for vision!
It's fairly certain they are not –
but let's give thanks for what we've got.

His crash

When James II lost his place,
Sam was retired in disgrace
because he didn't care to sign
on the proverbial dotted line
his bond to King William III.
The takeover that had occurred
did not, in Samuel's judgment, mean
that he should serve a King and Queen
who had displaced the rightful heir –
that was an oath he wouldn't swear.
He was, in many people's sight,
a Stuart man, a Jacobite,
and twice at least he went to gaol
(although his friends coughed up the bail).
He spent his last years quietly

in his enormous Library –
3,000 books, now housed within
his Cambridge college, Magdalene.[2]
It's here his Diary was found,
six volumes of it, neatly bound.
It was eventually translated,
the juicy bits emasculated,
and cut to 25 per cent
of its original extent;
and you may be surprised to know
that not till 30 years ago
did painstaking decoding dare
to lay *all* Samuel's secrets bare!

---

2   Pronounced 'Maudlin'

22

SIR ISAAC NEWTON

25 DECEMBER 1642 – 20 MARCH 1727

Who formulated the theory of gravity

Whether or not the Apple fell,
what made our hero Great
was seeing that the Moon, as well,
would like to gravitate

towards the Earth, but stays up high
on its celestial course.
And then he saw the reason why –
its *centrifugal force*!

This force would whirl the Moon away
into the depths of space,
but Gravity has made it stay
in its accustomed place.

(The Apple, if it could be hurled
with unexampled might,
would also zoom around the world –
a mini-satellite.)

He came up with the formulae
(a clever thing to do),
and also showed that Gravity
must grip the planets too.

But did this neat idea make sense?
How could attraction act
when distances were so immense?
And then there was the fact

that with the time that had elapsed
(if All attracted All),
the stars by now should have collapsed
into a solid ball!

Their speed, we know, keeps them apart;
but Newton thought them still.
So Gravity must stop and start
according to God's will!

That rational age had left behind
the medieval night,
and we can see his mighty mind
excited by the light

that Reason's blazing lantern shone.
But far beyond its shine
stretched wastes no one could look upon –
the realm of the Divine.

Don't be surprised to see him use
his cutting-edge IQ
to work out from the Bible's clues
when Jesus should be due!

Well, having put him in his place
(in a contextual way),
I haven't left myself much space.
So let me briefly say

Principia came off the press
in 1689.[1]
It was an overnight success.
In fact, it would define

---

1   Newton was cajoled into writing *Philosophiae Naturalis Principia Mathematica* by Edmund Halley (1656–1742).

the methods used to calculate
how bodies move through space
right up until the present date!
It only lost its place

with baffling relativistic stuff
that calls space curved, not flat.
But Newton had achieved enough –
he can't be blamed for that!

At 60 he resigned his Chair,[2]
and did a well-paid stint
with England's coinage in his care,
as Master of the Mint.

His final earthly stretch was marred
by a tremendous fuss –
a fight with Leibniz, no holds barred,
regarding Calculus.[3]

His rage at so-called enemies
was terrible to see;
but we forgive this fault of his,
and praise his Gravity.

---

2   He was elected to the Lucasian Chair of Mathematics at Cambridge
at the age of 27.

3   Gottfried Wilhelm Leibniz (1646–1716), philosopher and
mathematician, invented calculus independently of Newton, and his
notation is the one used today.

23.

JOHN CHURCHILL, 1ST DUKE OF MARLBOROUGH

26 MAY 1650 – 16 JUNE 1722

Winner and loser

John Churchill was a soldier bold,
and used to war's alarms.
He mused on Sarah Jennings' legs
and other hidden charms.

She needed all his skill to woo,
as his long siege would prove.
But winning her would be, John knew,
a good career move

for she was friends with Princess Anne –
a useful thing to be.
The wife of an ambitious man
should mix with royalty!

(Anne was King James II's daughter,
graced with the royal gene;
but nobody back then had thought her
a likely future Queen!)

King James raised John to topmost rank
when he was 38,
but when that monarch's rating sank,
John thought: 'For King or State?'

King William of the Netherlands
was asked to rule instead.
John put his troops in William's hands,
and James II fled.

Hedging his bets, John wrote to James
(who might return to power).
This letter, signed by several names,
meant five weeks in the Tower.

His head stayed on his shoulders, true;
but even so, our hero
lost all he'd been entitled to –
career prospects: zero!

When William died and left no heir,
Queen Anne began her reign.[1]
She'd promised Sarah: 'Don't despair –
John will be Great again!'

In weeks, his titles were restored.
Since we were fighting France
(as usual), he was sent abroad,
and seized his heaven-sent chance.

Mons, Blenheim, Toulon, Lille, Tournai,
Oudenarde, Ramillies;
the butchery of Malplaquet;
of victories like these

the Duke of Wellington (q.v.),
who'd won some battles, said:
'No greater army could there be
with Marlborough at its head!'

---

1   Anne reigned from 1702–1714.

A RHYMING HISTORY

So Blenheim Palace was begun –
his 'thank you' from the nation.
But money scandals soon began
to hurt his reputation.

They went abroad to dodge the flak
until the fuss had died.
But it was years after they got back
before they could reside

in Blenheim's partly-finished shell.
Lancelot Brown (q.v.)
landscaped the grounds, which he could tell
had 'capability'!

24

GEORGE FREDERICK HANDEL
23 FEBRUARY 1685 – 14 APRIL 1759

Who wrote a lot more than the Hallelujah Chorus

Handel was German-born, of course;
we Briticised him later.[1]
Bach said (according to one source)
that only Bach was greater!

He turned out operas by the score,
and oratorios too.
Let me explain a little more
what oratorios do...

They're always based on Holy Writ,
and tend to have a choir,
plus soloists who do their bit –
just think of the 'Messiah'!

He served the first two Georges' whim,
composing to their mood.
The pieces that were asked of him
(as you must know) include

the 'Water Music', played afloat
to please the King and Queen,
who partied in the royal boat
in 1717.

---

1   Handel was naturalised in 1727.

A Classic FM choice, I'd say!
His operas, however,
have worn less well, and most, today,
are rarely played, if ever.

Not so his oratorios,
which number 23;
a good half-dozen or more of those
are heard quite frequently.

This format, Handel introduced;
It caused a real stir.
The earliest one to be produced
was 'Esther'. After her

'Belshazzar', 'The Messiah', 'Saul',
and 'Samson' come to mind,
plus 'Jephtha', written last of all,
when he was going blind.

He passed away aged 74.
His grave cannot be missed.
He lies beneath the Abbey floor –
right by the organist!

25.

WILLIAM HOGARTH

10 NOVEMBER 1697 – 26 OCTOBER 1764

Who depicted the human condition

Hogarth started something new.
Not an easy thing to do
if you sell your Art to live –
people are conservative!
Still, he must have known or thought
that clients of the wealthier sort
would buy the pictures he engraved
that represented the depraved,
the foolish, or the sheer no-hopers
(such as the entertaining topers

in *Gin Lane*). He experimented
with sets of pictures, which presented
a story's stages (1... 2... 3...)
just like the Bayeux Tapestry.
These fairly bawdy sets of prints
have been sought after ever since.
In two examples, Hogarth makes
a *Harlot's Progress* (and a *Rake's*)
the subject of successive views
that show the pitfalls, should you choose
to slide down Virtue's slippery slope
(none of my readers will, I hope).
Another, *Marriage à la Mode*,
depicts an Earl with too much owed
espousing an heiress, which leads
to desperate and heinous deeds.
More episodes in his collection
include a most corrupt Election,
the just desserts of Idleness,
the side-effects of Drunkenness
(*Gin Lane*, to which I have alluded) –
in short, as you will have concluded,
he was a social commentator.
Dickens (q.v.) observed, much later,
the 'miserable reality'
that Hogarth drew so vividly
of London's poor. Soon, his engravings
were offered at substantial savings
by Pirates (proving his appeal);
such villains were allowed to steal
an artist's work, till MPs backed
what's rightly known as Hogarth's Act –
it meant that prints, as well as books,
could not be reproduced by crooks.
His gift for 'caricaturisation'
was certainly an inspiration

for Henry Fielding, his friend,[1]
who started a new reading trend –
the *novel*! Hogarth's influence
on literature was immense,
as well as focusing attention
on things it wasn't nice to mention.
'Hogarthian' (grotesque, absurd),
although a very useful word,
is not found in the dictionary –
but since it's used, it ought to be![2]

---

1   Henry Fielding (1707–1754) was the author of *Tom Jones*.
2   At least, it is not in my *Concise Oxford Dictionary* (8th Edition, 1990).

26.

JOHN WESLEY

17 JUNE 1703 – 2 MARCH 1791

Principal founder of the Methodist Church

Remember Wesley, when you're told
'The hymn is XYZ.'
Before his days,
the songs of praise
were sung by choirs instead.

He called to those beyond the Church –
the labourers who slaved
at plough or loom...
The Day of Doom
approached – they must be saved!

But not for him the pulpit, pew,
and preacher set on high.
His church would be
the scenery,
its roof the open sky.

His 40,000 eulogies[1]
explained what they must do.
'Open your heart –
let Jesus start
to show his love for you!'

---

1   An estimate of the number of meetings he addressed since the
     Methodists began their work in 1739.

The tenets of the C of E
he echoed, in the main;
but disagreed
about the need
for Bishops to ordain.

The so-called Apostolic Blessing
(he thought) did not make sense.
Lay preachers could
be just as good
at giving sacraments!

Since Bishops were supposed to hail
from Peter (or the Rock),
to say their line
was not divine
produced a seismic shock.

And on this rock, the churches split.
The Methodists departed...
But when you hymn,
remember him,
for that's when singing started!

27.

DR SAMUEL JOHNSON
7 SEPTEMBER 1709 – 13 DECEMBER 1784

Who compiled the first English dictionary

Not all these Greats, it has to be confessed,
would shine at dinner-table conversation;
but if I had the choice, I would suggest
that 'Doctor Johnson' gets an invitation!

This Lichfield lad struggled to make his way
by tutoring, translating and the like –
a real bore! Then came the happy day
when London called, and he got on his bike.

The Capital resounded to the clatter
as metal letters left their inky kiss,
rattling out quires of densely-printed matter
from ads to almanacs! Despite all this

the words imprinted by each merry press
were vague; nor had their spelling been agreed.
(One instance you will find in my PS.)
A *dictionary* was an urgent need!

So Samuel decided to embark
upon this monumental undertaking.
A labour of love, a leap into the dark;
and almost certainly non-profit-making.

Subscriptions raised the cash he thought he needed
(six drudges formed the workforce that he led).[1]
Funds kept on drying up as they proceeded;
it took nine years to get from A to Z,

when 40,000 words had been defined,
plus quotes to show their etymology;
and Oxford University opined
that this was worth a doctoral degree!

Eight years after the publication date,[2]
he met his boon companion and Narrator.
Although the Dictionary made Johnson Great,
James Boswell's *Life* would make him even Greater![3]

Postscript

A lady not burdened with tact,
told him: 'Doctor, you smell! That's a fact!'
He said: 'Madam, I think
you should say that I *stink*.
You're the person who *smells*! Be exact!'

---

1   His whimsical definition of 'lexicographer': 'A writer of dictionaries;
    a harmless drudge'.
2   *A DICTIONARY, with a Grammar and History, of the ENGLISH
    LANGUAGE,* 1755.
3   James Boswell (1740–1795) published his *Life of Johnson* in 1791.

28.

LANCELOT 'CAPABILITY' BROWN
C. 1716 – 6 FEBRUARY 1783

Who contrived natural prospects

The English garden underwent
a major change when William Kent[1]
(Brown's master) gave up tidy hedges,
and flower beds with gravelled edges.
Instead of the enclosed parterre
where everything is nice and square
(quite contrary to Nature's ways),
he spearheaded the English craze
for asking Nature: 'Let us see
if we can reach an amnesty.
Your trees are mostly misaligned;
your contours must be redesigned;
but it will seem au naturel
so far as visitors can tell!'
Brown got the setters of the trend
to rip out fences, and extend
their acres in a seamless sweep
enlivened by colluding sheep
(kept distanced by the ha-ha, which
was in effect a wall and ditch
that from the homestead didn't show).
Here one could wander to and fro,
or dally by an edifice

---

1   William Kent (*c.*1685–1748) was also an architect, who designed
      some of the buildings in Whitehall.

evoking lost Arcadian bliss,
or party by the new-made lake.
The change that 'Nature tamed' would make
is hard to credit, for we're used
to what the Age of Brown produced –
parks spreading off to the horizon
with focal points to rest our eyes on
('a typically English view'!)
At Warwick Castle, Blenheim, Kew,
and other places far and near,
you'll see how Landscape *should* appear
if only it were more aesthetic.
Brown was extremely energetic
in pushing these ideas of his:
almost 200 properties
had Nature very much improved
by all the earth his workers moved;
a careless river that was flowing
where water had no business going
was altered to another track,
and trees were planted by the sack.
(His famous nickname celebrates
his sales patter – all estates
were 'capable', as you'd expect,
once he had gone around and checked!)
Then Wordsworth came along (q.v.)...
Romantic sensibility
abhorred the thought of 'Nature tamed',
and Brown & Co. were roundly blamed
for prettifying Landscape thus,
which seemed to some quite barbarous.
Besides, the rising bourgeois class
did not own vast amounts of grass;
they wanted a herbaceous border
one gardener could keep in order,
as well as plots for fruit and veg,
enclosed within a wall or hedge.

We Brits now see those schemes of his
matured by two centuries.
To gaze on Brown's work helps us sense
the solid Georgian confidence
that made those mighty garden-makers
uplift or scrape down countless acres
and plant trees that they'd never see
achieve their full maturity.
The National Trust owns quite a few –
so join, and you can jump the queue!

29.

CAPTAIN JAMES COOK
27 OCTOBER 1728 – 14 FEBRUARY 1779

King George III's most assiduous explorer

1. He discovers Australia

He's ringed the globe, your Majesty – three years he's been away,
and he's dropped a new world, Sire, in your lap!
It will double your dominion
(that's good news, in our opinion).
Australia is the new name on the map!

He had sailed to Tahiti (which is pretty far away),
to observe the planet Venus cross the Sun,
in a coal-barque named *Endeavour*,
with no notion whatsoever
that he'd find a whole new world before he'd done.

2. He tries to find Antarctica

But there's one unanswered question, Sire, which hasn't gone away –
does a continent exist around the Pole?
In Cook's new ship *Resolution*
he will hunt for a solution.
It'll take three years, if they get through it whole!

Well, he got quite near the Pole (about twelve hundred miles away),
but to his chagrin, nothing came in view.[1]
Still, he found some other lands
to put into your hands,
like South Georgia, Sire, christened after you!

---

1   The first definite sighting of Antarctica was not made until 1820.

3. He hunts for the North-West Passage

He is on a Captain's pension, but he wants to get away,
so *Resolution*'s setting sail once more.
The North-West Passage beckons,
since he obstinately reckons
there's a route around the north-Canadian shore.

Past Good Hope he's gone again, and he slowly made his way
up America's west coast, which he surveyed.
But the Bering Strait was icy,
and the prospects much too dicey,
so Hawaii is the place for which he's made.

We are sorry, Sire, to say, that your explorer's passed away –
a native stabbed him in some altercation.
So they've buried him at sea,
which is where he liked to be –
but we wish you'd given him a decoration!

30.

EDMUND BURKE

12 JANUARY 1729 – 9 JULY 1797

Who believed in Difference, and proposed political parties

If you'd asked Edmund Burke
'Will Equality work?'
he would, I am sure, have said 'No!'
Today we are taught
that we're all of one sort;
Burke denied this, and so did Rousseau.[1]

The world's different races
have developed in places
that make their traditions unique.
Mother Nature decreed
that they loved their own breed;
so how could you possibly speak

of 'globalisation' –
the world's population
linked by equally intimate ties?
Burke would greatly prefer
to leave things as they were,
for in *difference* stability lies!

Each society, too,
will be (in his view)
divided by class and degree.
Making Britishers one
simply cannot be done,
without levelling downwards, i.e.

---

1   Jean-Jacques Rousseau (1712–1778) accepted natural inequality, but
     associated patronage and wealth with corruption.

reducing the best
to the state of the rest,
so our excellent standards will fall.
(You won't be surprised
that our Thinker advised
against giving the vote to us all!)

Still, this bold politician
took a front-line position
against the unprincipled folk
who could make MPs do
what they wanted them to.
Corruption was almost a joke,

for the landowners then
put up their own men
as MPs for the seats they controlled.
Which suited them fine
if their pawns toed the line
and voted the way they were told!

Burke was clearly distressed
that these Members were pressed
to oppose what their consciences urged.
They should speak what they thought,
and vote how they ought;
and so *parties* in due course emerged.

If he saw us today,
I expect Burke would say
that we're trying to fight 'evolution'
with increased legislation,
hamstringing the nation –
which is not, in his view, the solution!

31.

JAMES WATT
19 JANUARY 1736 – 19 AUGUST 1819

Whose steam engine powered the Industrial Revolution

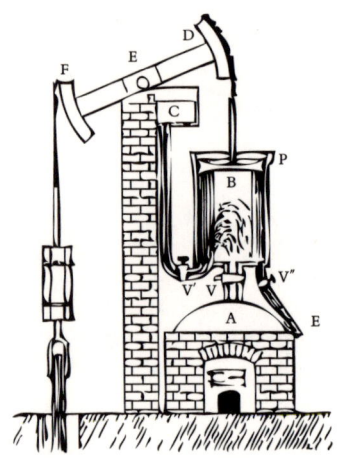

Let us celebrate Watt
(an ingenious Scot)
for the clever machine he designed.
With his brain he deduced...
with his hands he produced...
Inventor and Maker combined!

Initially, Watt
learned a hell of a lot
by repairing mechanical things.
He made instruments too –
the sort that you blew,
or enraptured by bowing the strings.

A RHYMING HISTORY

A repair job he'd got
was the reason for Watt
to reflect on Steam's massive potential.
And here I must mention
Newcomen's invention
(to refer to the sketch is essential).[1]

A weight below ground
pulled the beam 'E' around
anti-clockwise. It came to a stop

when the piston (marked 'P')
in the cylinder ('B')
had been carried right up to the top...

The next part of the scheme
was to fill 'B' with steam,
which was cooled by cold water, and shrank.
The pressure reduction
caused a powerful suction,
and 'E' turned with a deafening clank.

The problem, thought Watt,
lay in keeping things hot,
since the chamber was constantly chilled
for the steam to condense.
Which didn't make sense!
But if a *condenser* was filled

with the steam, it would not
(according to Watt)
cool the chamber – the engine would stay
as hot as it ought,
a leap forward, he thought,
compared with the Newcomen way!

---

1   Thomas Newcomen (1664–1729) devised the world's first practical
     steam engine.

Having thought of this, Watt
had his very first shot
at a model, which proved a success.
It had vastly more puff,
but this wasn't enough –
without backing, he couldn't progress.

His first backer left Watt
in a bit of a spot,
but the second was just what he needed –
a smelter of iron
he could really rely on.
The two agreed terms, and proceeded

to found Boulton & Watt.[2]
The resources he'd got
pushed their firm to the front of the queue.
On the factory floor,
pumping mines, crushing ore,
you'd find one of their engines (or two).

Oh, I almost forgot
to mention the watt –
named after our hero, of course.
But one watt is so small
it does nothing at all –
the unit he used was the 'horse'![3]

---

2   Matthew Boulton (1728–1809) entered into partnership with Watt in 1775.

3   Watt coined the term 'horsepower' in 1782. It is equivalent to 746 watts.

32.

THOMAS PAINE

29 JANUARY 1737–8 JUNE 1809

Who wrote Common Sense *(a handbook for the
American Revolution) and* The Rights of Man

Common Sense *is all you need,*
Yankee doodle dandy.
If you want a book to read,
keep a copy handy.[1]

I started as an exciseman.
Thought the pay was awful.
Got the sack for speaking out.
Told it was unlawful!

Marked down as a troublemaker.
Soon I started packing.
Sailed for the colonies.
The Yanks could use my backing!

Some states wished to keep the King.
Others said to sever.
I urged separation now,
on no terms whatsoever!

Wrote my views and published them.
Common Sense the title.
Really spelled the message out
(clarity was vital).

---

1   'Yankee Doodle Dandy' was a popular American revolutionary song.

Half a million copies sold.
Earned me lots of credit.
Washington said afterwards
it thrilled him when he read it!

France was starting to revolt.
Deeply ruminated...
Wrote my famous *Rights of Man*.
Made me celebrated.

Says we all have equal rights,
and rights should be respected.
Riled Edmund Burke (q.v.).
Just what I expected!

Bonaparte thought it was great.
Went right off him later.
The French were meant to rule themselves,
not get a new dictator!

Came back to the USA
(banned for life from Britain).
But people here aren't all that pleased
by other things I've written.

My *Age of Reason* tears to bits
the different creeds. Why claim
they speak to God exclusively?
To God, we're all the same!

That went down like a lead balloon,
at which I'm not surprised.
And then that Letter which I wrote![2]
It deeply criticised

---

2   *Letter to George Washington*, 1796

the USA's new government.
George Washington, I'd heard
was just as anti-common folk
as Britain's George III!

Will crowds escort me to my grave
when sexton tolls the bell?
Some hope! They'll smile as I pass
and hope I rot in hell.[3]

Thought that 'common sense' would do.
I was wrong, full-stop.
Two uprisings I've lived through,
and both have been a flop!

---

3   It is claimed that six mourners (including two freed slaves) went to his funeral. William Cobbett (1763–1835), a fellow-radical, brought his body back to England for ceremonial re-burial, but the bones were lost.

33

EDWARD JENNER

17 MAY 1749 – 26 JANUARY 1823

Who promoted the use of a vaccine for smallpox

One day, before noon,
Jenner launched a balloon
borne up by H_2
to see how it flew.
It started all right,
then began to lose height
as it travelled north-east,
till its journeying ceased
on the country estate
of the father of Kate,
ten miles away.
What more need I say?
Though the sight may have shocked her,
the engaging young doctor
who arrived to explain,
would be asked back again...

Jenner's fertile mind
was eager to find
more things to pursue (!) –
and he found quite a few...
When exploring, he saw
a plesiosaur
(the earliest known)
embedded in stone,
which he chiselled and hacked,
convinced of the fact

that such things were long gone,
and the world had moved on –
though few would agree
before Darwin (q.v.).

Jenner studied, as well,
how that orphan from hell
(the Cuckoo, of course)
disinherits by force
the parents' own brood
and gets fed all the food.
He learned that the chick
does this mischievous trick
of its inner volition...[1]
But soon our physician
had started to wonder:
'Why don't milkmaids go under
when smallpox appears?'
It was rife in those years,
and cut the lives short
of a third that it caught,
while the rest remained scarred.
Edward thought very hard...
All the milkmaids he knew
had a blister or two
from the cowpox, suggesting
that this was arresting
the dreaded disease!
Jenner managed to squeeze
some pus from inside,
which he duly applied
to a boy, as a test.

---

[1]   This was disputed until the evidence of photography. It had been
      assumed that the parents evicted the rightful tenants.

The result can be guessed –
the patient fell ill
(as people do still),
but improved very soon
and was henceforth immune
to later injections
of related infections!
Some already suspected
that a person infected
with cowpox, did not
have to worry a lot
with the smallpox about;
but there's no room for doubt
that Edward's the one
who had really begun
researching away
until he could say
that cowpox *had* been
an effective vaccine.
This persuaded the State
to vote funds for our Great
to keep on injecting
in the hope of perfecting
a convenient jab
in his up-to-date lab.
I'll end with a thought
of a sobering sort:
if he hadn't persisted,
would your line have existed?

34.

WILLIAM BLAKE

28 NOVEMBER 1757 – 12 AUGUST 1827

Visionary, poet and artist

William, did you get a fright
at your first celestial sight?
Did it throw you, to espy,
up a tree in Peckham Rye,
angels thronging every bough?[1]
(They are rarely seen there now.)
Did this sight of heaven on earth

---

1   This experience is supposed to have occurred to him when he was
     between eight and ten.

make you reassess your worth?
'Tyger, Tyger' (which you wrote)
ends on a bewildered note,
wondering if God foresaw
the power of this predator;
did the Peckham angels say
that we are more than living clay?
If we are, then does it mean
that when the rising sun is seen
we should perceive a heavenly choir,
and not a distant orb of fire?
William, is it true you thought
that revelations of this sort
were a glimpse of Light denied
to fearful minds that never tried
to try Imagination's door
in case it opened, and they saw
what they'd been told they could not see,
by Doctors of Theology?

He was reckoned crazy then
by many of his fellow-men,
for warning of too much reliance
on *explanation* (i.e. Science),
which distanced us from Revelation
by down-grading imagination.
Are things different today?
Who reads William anyway,
except for purple passages
included in anthologies?
Why was he adjudged so Great,
and placed at No. 38
when listed by the BBC?
The answer lies, it seems to me,
in two short poems. First of all
'The Tyger', framed upon the wall;

and then the song that's taken root
within the Women's Institute,
and should be bellowed out by them
each time they meet – 'Jerusalem'
(although some rebel groups, I fear,
have cut it down to once a year).
These compositions, I suggest,
are how his Greatness was assessed,
and why his vogue remains so high
beyond the bounds of Peckham Rye.

35.

HORATIO, LORD NELSON
29 SEPTEMBER 1758 – 21 OCTOBER 1805

Our greatest naval commander

Here's to the name of the highest of all –
at least in a metrical sense.
He was twelve when the sea began to call,
and he died in our defence.
But his stomach deplored its time aboard,
no matter how steady the boat;
he was sick as a dog on the sea he adored
throughout his life afloat!
His eye was smashed beyond repair,
and his arm was blown to bits.
But he's up in the air in Trafalgar Square,
way above all the rest of the Brits!

He was 20 years old, on a captain's pay,
when he sailed off west to suppress
the up-and-coming USA –
and he didn't have much success.
For the war was hopeless from the start
(the task was Herculean),
though he did win Fanny Nisbet's heart
while in the Caribbean![1]
Oh, his eye was smashed beyond repair,
and his arm was blown to bits.
But he's up in the air in Trafalgar Square,
way above all the rest of the Brits!

---

1   They married in 1787, but had no children. He had a daughter,
        Horatia, by Emma Hamilton.

Long tedious years on land ensued,
till French ambition stirred.
They claimed Spain for their own in belligerent mood,
and had to be deterred.
So he sailed to the Med, and here he beat
(at the Battle of the Nile)[2]
the whole of Napoleon Bonaparte's fleet,
which stunned Boney for a while!
True, his eye was smashed beyond repair,
and his arm was blown to bits.
But he's up in the air in Trafalgar Square,
way above all the rest of the Brits!

To Naples he went, and he met his match
in an even more glittering prize,
for this was Lady Hamilton's patch,
and they dazzled each other's eyes.
Great men had mistresses – so what?
(Such things were de rigueur.)
But he ought to be discreet, and not
live openly with her!
Yes, his eye was smashed beyond repair,
and his arm was blown to bits.
But he's up in the air in Trafalgar Square,
way above all the rest of the Brits!

He was fighting the renegade Danish lot,
when a signal was displayed
saying: 'Break off the action – it's getting too hot,'
but it *couldn't* be obeyed![3]
So he put his glass to his blinded eye,
and muttered: 'I cannot see
any signal at all.' And that is why

---

2   1–2 August 1798
3   Battle of Copenhagen, 2 April 1801

he won the victory!
Sure, his eye was smashed beyond repair,
and his arm was blown to bits.
But he's up in the air in Trafalgar Square,
way above all the rest of the Brits!

So we come at last to Trafalgar Day,[4]
when the French are seen in force,
and he says to his men what he has to say,
which is, 'England expects,' of course!
A sniper's shot goes through his chest,
and there's nothing they can do;
but he knows that the Brits have come off best,
and he's done his duty too!
So now he's smashed beyond repair,
and he bows his head at last.
But his spirit is there in Trafalgar Square
to remind us of our past!

---

4   21 October 1805

36

ROBERT BURNS

25 JANUARY 1759 – 21 JULY 1796

Scotland's national poet

Did Rabbie have a red, red nose
from all the scotch he drank?
He may have later, I suppose,
with money in the bank!

Brought up a servant to the plough,
his father works him hard,
but makes him read – that's why he's now
considered Scotland's Bard.

At 15, Rabbie pens some lines
addressed to 'Handsome Nell'.
With women, he shows all the signs
of doing very well.

To grow sufficient food to eat,
our versifier tries
to carry on and make ends meet
after his father dies,

by moving to Mossgiel, near Ayr.
His future wife, Jean Armour,
is one of the attractions there.
He very soon disarms her,

and in due time she bears him twins.
He thinks of emigration,
but suddenly his life begins –
he's offered publication!

His Poems in the Dialect
become an instant hit.[1]
The 'Ploughman Poet' wins respect –
and earns a tidy bit!

He notes down Scottish songs he hears,
and writes more of his own –
creating in the next five years
the ones for which he's known...

Like 'Red, Red Rose' and 'Scots Wha Hae',
as well as 'Banks and Braes';
and 'Auld Lang Syne' for New Year's Day.
But this productive phase

is clouded by his loud approval
of France's Reign of Fear.
Their King and Queen's abrupt removal
does not go down well here!

Few poets, then or now, can boast
that rhyming really pays.
The Excise offer him a post
in Dumfries, where he stays

until his brief life's story ends.
His health has now declined;
his views have cost him many friends,
and he is too inclined

---

1   *Poems, Chiefly in the Scottish Dialect*, 1786

to down a thimble of the stuff
that fires the Scottish will.
At 37 he's drunk enough,
and Rabbie's pen is still!

But on the twenty-fifth of Jan.,
wherever they may be,
Scots toast the Haggis and the Man,
and down a dram (or three).

37

WILLIAM WILBERFORCE

24 AUGUST 1759 – 29 JULY 1833

Who fought for better morals and an end to the slave trade

This reformer saw two goals to work for (at least),
though his eyesight was not of the best.
Nor was he robust, and his stooping increased
till his head was bowed down on his chest.

His father had flourished on overseas trade...
Young William became an MP
when just 20 years old, and a Member he stayed
till St Peter (we hope) turned the key!

He managed to cut an acceptable dash
with the setters of fashion and trends
till he reached 26, when he saw in a flash
that he ought to start making amends.

Should he give up his seat, and embark on a mission
to propagate Goodness and Light?
He decided instead that his present position
would help with his forthcoming fight...

A cleric, James Ramsay, had written a tract
which examined the state of the ships
in which lucrative African labour was packed
for their West Indies sugar cane trips.

A RHYMING HISTORY

William Pitt (Britain's youngest PM) was his friend,
and told William he ought to campaign
to bring this unsavoury trade to an end,
though he wasn't the first to complain.

An Act was already about to be passed
reducing the crowding somewhat.
But to stop it left sweet-toothed opinion aghast –
the labour had *got* to be got!

So a group of reformers already existed
(Thomas Clarkson had marshalled their data);[1]
but William kept urging the House, and persisted
till the trade was banned 20 years later.

Meanwhile, his bright evangelical beam
lit up other dark corners as well.
He thought goodness should show, for it's how people *seem*
that inspires the rest to excel![2]

But he didn't just aim at the propertied few
with the time and the means to Improve.
The exploitable masses were God's children too,
and in 1802 he helped move

an Act of Employment, which started the cause
which Shaftesbury took up (q.v.),
to improve workers' hours by bringing in laws;
though it took a long time, as we'll see.

---

1   Thomas Clarkson (1760–1846) was as active as William in the cause.
     In one year alone he rode some 50,000 km collecting evidence, and
     survived a murderous attack.
2   *A Practical View of the Prevailing Religious System of Professed Christians
     in the Higher and Middle Classes of This Country, Contrasted with Real
     Christianity*, 1797.

In 1807, the slave trade was stopped;
but it's certain that many more died
when the Law came in sight, and the wretches were dropped
overboard, on the opposite side.

Twenty-six years went by, and he lay at death's door,
when a further enactment was passed
to free all the slaves who'd been press-ganged before;
and the struggle was over at last.

38.

ARTHUR WELLESLEY, 1ST DUKE OF WELLINGTON

1 MAY 1769 – 14 SEPTEMBER 1852

Who fought many battles against the French, including Waterloo

'What *can* I do with Arthur?' cries his mother in dismay.
'He hasn't any aptitude at all!
The Army is, I fear,
the only viable career.'
So Ensign Wellesley has himself a ball...

He falls in love with Kitty, but her parents say 'No way!
That worthless fellow's not the one you're choosing!'[1]
Apparently, the shock
makes him sit up and take stock –
he will work at soldiering, instead of boozing...

The European mainland is in utter disarray
now the French have guillotined their King and Queen.
The leaders of the nation
are intent on Subjugation
to create the greatest empire ever seen!

Napoleon's ambition will make Arthur's name one day,
but the Brits are busy subjugating too.
To India he's sent,
deploys his regiment,
and does the job that he is paid to do...

---

1   Catherine Pakenham 1772–1831

It's 13 years since he proposed; now Kitty's parents say
that she can be his wife, since he's much better.
They're not bound by any law,
but he pledged his heart before,
so he offers to espouse her, in a letter.

She delightedly accepts; but when he meets his fiancée,
he's staggered when he sees what Time has done.
They are married, all the same;
but despite his growing fame,
their ménage will never be a happy one.

The French have entered Spain, and they *must* be held at bay
(it's the height of the Napoleonic Era).
Arthur, plus the Portuguese,
win great battles such as these:
Vimeneia, Poliçe, and Talavera,

Torres Vedras and Badajoz. Six years he is away,
and the War in the Peninsula goes on
till his overall success
makes him Viscount, then Marquess,
and ultimately *Duke* of Wellington!

With Napoleon on Elba, peace has surely come to stay?
But he finds a boat, and France flares up again.
Arthur thinks the thing to do
is to head for Waterloo[2]
with approximately 70,000 men!

Napoleon *must* attack him, and the fight goes on all day.
Blücher's Prussians should be there as his reserves.
But there's not a sign of them
until almost 8 p.m. –
'It was a damned nice thing,' Arthur observes...

---

2   Battle of Waterloo, 18 June 1815

He's gratefully ennobled, so he puts his sword away
and enters politics. But he's attacked
for trying to prevent
enhanced enfranchisement –
the thought of 'people power' does not attract!

He is called the 'Iron Duke' because he wanted to delay
the movement for Reform, when Robert Peel
got the famous measure passed;[3]
so although he lost at last,
let's recall his battles, won by nerves of Steel!

---

3   Peel was the prime minister when the 1832 Reform Act was passed.

39

WILLIAM WORDSWORTH
7 APRIL 1770 – 23 APRIL 1850

Our greatest Romantic poet

1. Revolution (1790)

'Bliss was it in that dawn to be alive,'
he wrote, 'but to be young was very heaven!'
These lines he set down in 1805,
and published in *The Prelude*, Book XI –
he'd gone to France, then gripped in revolution,
excited by the bold experiment.
Like Locke (q.v.), he thought it the solution –
remove the King, have grass-roots government!
He met Annette Vallon; they had a daughter,
but never married, though he did support her.

2. The *Lyrical Ballads* (1798)

His sister Dorothy and he
enjoyed unusual harmony,
and went to live in Somerset,
near Coleridge (whom he had met).[1]
The two men shared the same ideas;
a new poetic form appears,
known as 'Romantic'. In their eyes,
the tendency to analyse,
to measure, and to try to find
what goes on in Our Maker's mind

---

1   Samuel Taylor Coleridge, 1772–1834

creates a negative effect –
he wrote: 'We murder to dissect'![2]
The *Ballads* (their collaboration)
include his visceral sensation
when Tintern Abbey came in view.
The Ancient Mariner's there too,
which came from Coleridge's pen.
But they did not collude again,
for Wordsworth couldn't quite agree
with opium-based poetry.

3. Fame!

And so, off to the Lakeland hills
to wander lonely as a cloud
and gaze upon the daffodils –[3]
five children made it quite a crowd!
He took Dove Cottage on a lease,
lived with his sister and his wife,
and worked upon his masterpiece
The Prelude – it's about his life.
His output from then on was vast
(no one has read it all, I'll bet),
and in his sixties, he at last
received the crown of Laureate!

4. His legacy

'The world is too much with us,' he decided,[4]
and chose to live where wild things resided.
He was not of his time, much less of ours;
yet over all his rivals he still towers!

---

2   'The Tables Turned', 1798.
3   'I Wandered Lonely as a Cloud', 1807
4   'The World is Too Much With Us', 1807

Is that because we still retain a sense
of something lost, of lack of innocence?
Should we be more concerned with what fulfils?
Should we spend more time seeking daffodils?

40.

JOSEPH MALLORD
WILLIAM TURNER

c. 23 APRIL 1775 – 19 DECEMBER 1851

Painter of Light

His father, who barbered,
saw the gifts the boy harboured,
and drawings by Turner
proved a nice little earner
in his shop near the Thames.
One of Art's apophthegms,
that he Painted With Light,
must go back to the sight
of the River near home
(he could see St Paul's dome)
when the rising sun broke
through the steam and the smoke
and the aerial vapour,
which he'd jot down on paper
or mentally docket.
He rose like a rocket!
The Academy's taste
for landscape views based
on our infinite store
of mythical lore
was one he shared too;
it's a theme that runs through
to his last exhibition.
His famous rendition
of Ulysses scorning

Polyphemus one morning
in the course of his trips
(Turner loved painting ships)[1]
shows a trend he'd begun
where he looks *at* the sun
through the vaporous haze;
its eye-level rays
give the dazzling effect
that we've come to expect
in the works we know best!
Profoundly impressed
by the force of the squall
when barometers fall,
his late works start showing
rain raining, snow snowing,
rocks rocking, waves waving...
i.e. Nature behaving
in a challenging way.
I'm sorry to say
that the terms Turner willed
remain unfulfilled –
the plan in his mind
was a building designed
to contain his collection
for public inspection
(his gift to the nation
exceeds valuation).
So the best you can do
if you're anxious to view
the work of this Great
is to go to the Tate.

---

1   *Ulysses deriding Polyphemus*, 1829 (National Gallery).

41

JANE AUSTEN

16 DECEMBER 1775 – 18 JULY 1817

An enduring novelist

Although a country rector's daughter,
some suitors did attempt to court her,
to one of whom, we understand,
Jane offered her undowered hand;
but having died before he should,
our heroine chose spinsterhood.
She closed the door and wrote away
at secret hours of the day,
for novels weren't considered quite
the thing for maiden aunts to write!

Six books were the result of this,
including *Pride and Prejudice*,
about the stress a mother faced
in getting all five daughters placed
without a penny to their name
(the theme is more or less the same
in *Sense and Sensibility*).
Impoverished gentility,
the marriage market, and a way
of making her creations say
the opposite of what they feel
are Austen's trademark and appeal –
'ironic', 'pointed', even 'bitter'
are epithets that seem to fit her.
It's usual, when her work's assessed,
to pick out *Emma* as the best.
Her heroine's a marriage broker;
from time to time we'd like to choke her
when she manipulates and schemes,
but she is better than she seems,
and finally her heart is snared –
a course for which she's not prepared!
Jane Austen's scalpel disinters
the motives of her characters,
and though her age is so remote,
her insights strike a modern note.
At Winchester you'll find her bones;
her books are all in Waterstone's.

42

ELIZABETH GURNEY FRY

21 MAY 1780 – 12 OCTOBER 1845

Prison reformer and women's advocate

Elizabeth Fry
(no one could deny)
was a lady of strong motivation.
And being a Quaker
meant nothing could shake her;
so with that, I'll begin my laudation...

Elizabeth Gurney
began her life's journey
as a show-off. She'd deck herself out
in bright colours, which were
by no means de rigueur
in the eyes of the Quaker devout![1]

But it still appears odd
that she didn't meet God
until she was almost eighteen,
when a passionate preacher
let the Lord at last reach her,
and she saw what His blessing could mean.

She eschewed green and red,
turned 'plain Quaker' instead,
and married a banker called Fry.
She produced, as a mother,
one after another –
eleven all told! She wrote: 'Why

---

[1] The Gurney family of Norwich, with their ostentatious ways, did
not please their neighbouring 'plain Quakers'.

is my life, day by day,
simply slipping away?'
Well, soon after, the answer arrived!
Although she'd been preaching,
and doing some teaching,
in the Workhouses for the Deprived,

a visitor said,
'You are needed instead
by the women in Newgate. They're lying
without any straw
on the icy-cold floor,
and the babies they're bearing are dying!'

So, fired with zeal
by this heartfelt appeal,
Fry set out the very next day.
The turnkeys said 'Ma'am,
you may come to some harm!'
But she ordered them: 'Out of my way!'

The women's condition
decided her mission;
she not only worked for the cause
of Prison Reform,
but refuted the norm
by which *men* were in charge and made laws!

Not everyone thought
that the gospel she taught
was making their lives any better.
The prisoners found
that when Fry was around,
her Law must be kept to the Letter...

And her Rule No. 1
(in a nutshell, *No Fun*)
left them nothing to do with their leisure.
No gambling or drinking;
let the Book guide your thinking,
for the route to Corruption is Pleasure...

But to those of her gender,
her energies lend her
a pioneer status today.
Fry was first to succeed
in attacking the creed
that women are meant to obey!

43.

GEORGE STEPHENSON
9 JUNE 1781 – 12 AUGUST 1848

Builder of the first successful steam locomotive

With scarce a penny in his pocket
(from mining folk he came),
inventive George was due to rocket
to fortune and to fame.

He wasn't quite the first to see
that Steam could be the thing
to move a load from A to B.
There'd been some murmuring

when Hedley's *Puffing Billy* ran
along an iron line
(no faster than a walking man)
near Newcastle on Tyne.[1]

George knew that wasn't fast enough.
His first attempt could haul
some 30 tons – but lacked the puff
to do much more than crawl.

So nobody was that impressed –
a horse was quicker-moving!
Still, George was sure that steam was best.
His engines kept improving,

---

1   Built by William Hedley (1773–1843), *Puffing Billy* took to the rails
    in 1813.

until he heard about a scheme
to build the SDR –[2]
a *nine-mile* line! Could Smoke and Steam
pull anything this far?

The shareholders at last agreed
that horses were outmoded,
and George was ordered to proceed.
The *Locomotion*, loaded

with 80 tons of freight behind,
did what it had to do.
It even pulled a coach designed
to carry *humans* too.

The *Rocket* was his tour de force,[3]
and needs no words from me.
It's at South Kensington, of course –
and you can get in free!

---

2   The Stockton & Darlington Railway, which opened in 1825.
3   The *Rocket* was built for the Liverpool and Manchester
     Railway (1830).

MICHAEL FARADAY

22 SEPTEMBER 1791 – 25 AUGUST 1867

Electromagnetic pioneer

A lively and enquiring mind;
upbringing of the poorest kind;
he made his luck, as we shall find,
did Michael Faraday!

Bookbinding should have been his niche,
but reading what he ought to stitch
widened his knowledge greatly, which
encouraged him to pay

to join the crowds that flocked to see
experiments in Chemistry
by Humphry Davy. It was he[1]
whom Michael told, one day

about his optimistic dream.
'I'd really like to join your team –
I've jotted notes down by the ream!'
Sir Humphry said: 'OK!'

For almost two decades he stayed
both under-stretched and under-paid;
his master may have been afraid
he'd take his place, one day!

---

1   Sir Humphry Davy (1778–1829), noted chemist and physicist, was
     famous for his public lectures at the Royal Institution.

A RHYMING HISTORY

When Davy died, he could commence
the physical experiments
that made him such an influence,
especially the way

a magnet, moving rapidly
created electricity
within adjacent circuitry
(though why, he couldn't say).

From this, as everyone must know,
he came up with the Dynamo!
The Queen required him to go
to see her. 'Tell me, pray

why this is more than just a toy
to entertain the hoi polloi?'
'Ma'am, what use is a new-born boy
(or girl)?' asked Faraday...

45.

ANTHONY ASHLEY COOPER (LORD SHAFTESBURY)

28 APRIL 1801 – 1 OCTOBER 1885

Who fought for exploited children

Philanthropy (affection for mankind)
was rarely seen two centuries ago
in those who profited where coal was mined,
or from the shuttle's endless to-and-fro
inching our woolly treasure from the loom
in Britain's heady economic boom!

Such exploitation of the young and weak
made Shaftesbury a friend of the oppressed.
Our Saviour's chosen image, poor and meek,
proved that in God's eyes, humbleness was best.
Instead of boosting their employers' worth,
they ought to be inheriting the earth!

Children in mines, children up chimney flues...
The martyrs of industrialisation
needed a voice; his power he would use
to see about improving legislation.
Other reformers also backed the cause,
but Shaftesbury would pioneer the laws.

The first of many measures he suggested
limited children to a 10-hour day.
His Factories Bill was bitterly contested,

the owners making sure things went their way.
But on one thing they did at last agree:
you must be nine to work machinery.[1]

The Coal Mines Act of 1842;
the Ten-Hour Bill that followed three years later;
other reforms Lord Shaftesbury hustled through,
thanks partly to his growing store of data...
His ceaseless labour helped the young a lot –
but since they couldn't read or write, so what?

This thought inspired the Ragged Schools campaign[2]
for workers willing to be educated
(admirers, though, would frequently complain
that classrooms could be better ventilated).
These went on till the House of Commons backed
the 1870 Education Act.

In Piccadilly Circus, in his name,
a shrine was built in 1893.
It shows a wingèd archer, taking aim –
Anteros, symbolising Charity.
'Eros', the name on which the guides insist,
still celebrates this great Philanthropist!

---

1   Factories Act, 1833
2   Founded 1844

46

ISAMBARD KINGDOM BRUNEL
9 APRIL 1806 – 15 SEPTEMBER 1859

Who built to last

I'd never have reckoned
that Brunel would come *second*
in the BBC trawl
through the Best Brits of all!
It just shows the appeal
of Iron and Steel,
and our native delight
(when things turn out right)
in Vision and Drive.
Of his works that survive,
the Tamar Bridge still
gives the gazer a thrill –
such Euclidean grace,
like a theorem in space
(and do let me mention
the Avon Suspension,
though the gorge wasn't spanned
by the lacework he'd planned
until after he'd died.)
Brunel's father had tried,
by working non-stopping,
to tunnel to Wapping
from the opposite shore
by hoping to bore
beneath the Thames mud,
though it tended to flood;
the Son got it finished

as Dad's gusto diminished.[1]
But long before then
this most focussed of men
commenced his career
as Chief Engineer
(then aged 27)
to join London and Devon
by the Great Western link,
as we stood on the brink
of the Age of the Train!
To show his disdain
for conventional thought,
Brunel felt that he ought
to make the gauge wide,
which would cushion the ride;
but he'd hardly got laying
when he started displaying
an interest in trips
to New York (using ships).
The *Great Western* would show
how fast it could go
on the first voyage it made
using steam as an aid;
with both paddles churning
it clanked westwards, returning
in four weeks all told.
But Brunel broke the mould
with *Great Britain*, which set
the fastest time yet
with a hull made of iron;
and he chose to rely on
a *propeller* to drive her!

---

1   Sir Marc Brunel (1769–1849). The Tunnel was completed in 1843,
     after 18 years of work.

This noble survivor,
which was rusting away,
rests at Bristol today.
The *Great Eastern*, still vaster
(a commercial disaster),
showed no hope of a profit;
but they ripped the decks off it,
leaving space to enable
a submarine cable
to be winched out and sunk
in its casing or 'trunk'
so that London could talk
by Morse code to New York![2]
But Brunel never knew
what his 'baby' would do,
for he died of a stroke
before it puffed smoke.
Which brings something to mind...
Brunel was inclined
(like our No. 1 Brit)
to cigars, which he lit
at a furious speed –
a bad habit indeed!
So a photograph showing
the offending thing glowing
as he stands at his peak
was cleaned up, so to speak,
by removing all trace
of the object, in case
its use on a book
made schoolteachers say 'Look!
Role-models must be
squeaky-clean and vice-free;

---

2   This was the first successful transatlantic cable, laid in 1865.

if this Smoker's acclaimed,
can children be blamed
if they puff a cigar?
This is going too far!'[3]
So the brush was applied –
and the bad habit died...

---

3   *The Life of Isambard Kingdom Brunel*, published by Heinemann, 2005.

47.

JOHN STUART MILL
20 MAY 1806 – 8 MAY 1873

Who advocated Liberty and Happiness

John Stuart Mill was kept away
from boys as young as he.
His father knew he couldn't play
and study properly!

At three, his Greek was just so-so;
it's shocking to relate
how little Plato he would know
until the age of eight!

Worse, Aristotle stayed unread
while four more years went by.
Then something broke inside his head –
I can't imagine why.

By reading Wordsworth's rhymes (q.v.)
he pulled through. Then he met
a married woman, Mrs T.
(we'll call her Harriet)

with whom he'd happily debate
his liberal ideas.
They did not stain her married state
for more than twenty years!

Then Mr T. expired at last,
and Mill and she were wed.
A few delightful years went past –
then Harriet was dead.

That's very sad, you'll doubtless say;
but what's his claim to fame?
Two principles survive today
and celebrate his name...

The first, called *Liberty*, addressed
the common person's right
to act unhindered by the rest.
Completely so? 'Not quite,'

said J. S. Mill. 'Consider first
if they'll do others harm.
If not, then let them do their worst –
there's no cause for alarm!'

The Church, of course, did not agree.
An obvious deduction
from this degree of Liberty
is legal self-destruction!

The problem's fairly obvious –
how should 'harm' be defined?
J. S. assumed that all of us
are basically inclined

to ponder where our duties lie,
and not get into fights.
Free speech would be his rallying cry –
but what if it incites?

He also wrote on moral sense...
As an *empiricist*
(who judges by experience)
he tended to resist

laws made in Heaven, which decree
what's right and wrong. Instead,
Mill moralised pragmatically.
'Consider this,' he said.

'If what you do adds to the score
of happiness or pleasure
by bringing smiles to more and more,
you're Moral, by my measure!'

Utilitarianism, it's called.
Some tricky points were raised...
The Church was once again appalled –
pleasure should *not* be praised!

Much law now rests on his foundation...
When you have had your fill
of more and more 'rights' legislation,
just blame John Stuart Mill!

48.

CHARLES ROBERT DARWIN
12 FEBRUARY 1809 – 19 APRIL 1882

Who proposed evolution through natural selection

In large parts of the USA
Charles Darwin's name is mud today
for saying that the human race
mutated to its primal place.
Minds anchored to the Bible's text
are not unnaturally vexed;
they much prefer a master plan
with one sure outcome – i.e. Man!

His grandfather, Erasmus, thought
that evolution of a sort
produced our flora and our fauna,
with Mankind just around the corner.
So heresy was in his genes!
His father, who had ample means
(thanks to a wealthy clientele
who called him when they felt unwell)
intended him to be a priest,
which didn't tempt him in the least;
but then an offer came his way
to board the *Beagle*, and survey
the South American coast. From this
emerged the great hypothesis
that rocked the Church from east to west,
and by some sects is still suppressed...
Take *mockingbirds* as an example.
When he compared his careful sample
from different islands where they went,
the groups were slightly different,
and were, apparently, unique.
Did God give each first pair a tweak
when he created them on-site
(most pulpits took this view), or might
the different species have *evolved*?
Once back in England, he resolved
to study what was called Mutation –
a strange deep-seated variation
between the parent and the child,
which sometimes happens in the wild.
Most of these freaks do not succeed,
and die out; but if one should breed
a strain with more disease resistance
than those already in existence,
or won more tussles when it fought,
it would supplant the previous sort.

Forget about Divine Direction –
rely on Natural Selection!

The Origin of Species hit
the bookshops... Clerics had a fit![1]
The outcry wasn't unexpected.
Had *we* been Naturally Selected?
Had *we* descended from the trees
when our begetters, chimpanzees,
transmuted into things like us?
There was a God-Almighty fuss!
Well, now it makes much better sense,
but may I offer one defence
of those who claim they've been Created
and not just randomly mutated?
This question puzzles me a lot...
If we have souls, and apes do not,
did souls *evolve*? Or did God say:
'You'll never die – as from today!'?

---

1   He spent 20 years working on his theory before he published
On the Origin of Species in 1859.

ALFRED, LORD TENNYSON
6 AUGUST 1809 – 6 OCTOBER 1892

A popular Poet Laureate

A poet of the High Victorian Age,
the works of Tennyson were all the rage;
today, however, much of what he wrote
seems mannered, sentimental and remote –
much less approachable, if you ask me,
than Wordsworth, who pre-dated him (q.v.).
'The Lady of Shalott', which was a hit,
I have adapted for my fifth Great Brit
(King Arthur); and his *Idylls of the King*
(that's Arthur also) sold like anything.
The Light Brigade's heroic liquidation[1]
inspired his most famous peroration –
apparently he'd penned its thumping rhymes
an hour after opening *The Times*,
while 'In Memoriam', his noblest piece,
composed as an emotional release
when Arthur Hallam died (a Cambridge friend),
took 17 years before he'd reached the end.
He lived in comfort on the Isle of Wight,
and would be called to Osborne, to recite
to Queen Victoria, his reclusive neighbour.
She recognised the fruits of his life's labour
(including 'Come into the garden, Maud')
by making Alfred Tennyson a Lord.

---

[1]   'The Charge of the Light Brigade', a tribute to those who fought at
        the Battle of Balaclava during the Crimean War, on 25 October 1854.

50.

CHARLES JOHN HUFFAM DICKENS

7 FEBRUARY 1812 – 9 JUNE 1870

A great popular novelist

He wrote five million words, at least!
As each instalment was released
his popularity increased;
and even though he's long deceased,
he's still a household name!

His upbringing was pretty fraught,
if we can go by his report.
His father, who was always short,
was sentenced in a debtors' court.
His mother got the blame

for making Charles an employee
at Warren's Blacking Factory,
with waifs and strays as poor as he!
This unremitting purgatory
inspired in him the aim

of bettering his occupation.
He wrote a book, whose publication
was nothing short of a sensation –
The Pickwick Papers hit the nation
and brought him instant fame!

A RHYMING HISTORY

His output was unprecedented.
No other author has invented
such characters as he presented
(grotesque, pathetic, or demented) –
no two of them the same!

With destitution everywhere,
Dickens was very much aware
of how unfettered laissez-faire
denied the poor their proper share
of what they ought to claim.

Compassion, yes; upheaval, no!
The high stayed high, the low stayed low.
He wouldn't change the status quo –
he was Victorian, you know!
For that, he's not to blame.

He was a writer of his day
who wrote the books he thought would pay.
His life and times have passed away,
but Oliver & Co. will stay –
like him, a household name!

51

DR DAVID LIVINGSTONE
19 MARCH 1813 – 1 MAY 1873

Who tried to bring Light to Africa

'Christianity, Commerce, and Civilisation'
are inscribed on his monument's base.[1]
It couldn't be clearer
that he lived in an era
when the Brits had no doubt of their place!

Blantyre, near Glasgow, is where he was born,
and off to the mill he was sent.
His father sold tea
evangelically,
giving tracts out wherever he went.

Being born with a brain that was anxious for facts,
David studied from morning till night.
It is said that he read
while spinning the thread;
but he didn't encounter the Light

until 20 years old, when he suddenly felt,
like Thomas Barnardo (q.v.),
that the Chinese could do
with a preacher or two,
so he worked for his doctor's degree.

---

1   His monument by the Victoria Falls, which he first sighted on 17
     November 1855

But the Opium War meant that travel was off...[2]
Dr Moffat, a fellow Scot, said
that South Africa's races
were desperate cases,
and perhaps he should go there instead?

The first eight years there (he remained for 16)
were spent setting up schools in the Bush.
But the Whites were dismayed:
'If they *learn*, we're afraid
we might end up by getting the push!'

So David decided he'd better *explore*
and evangelise as he proceeded.
If things worked out as planned,
he would annexe more land
and bring Jesus to where he was needed!

This included a trudge from the west to the east –
from Angola to Mozambique's coast.
Nearly two years it took,
while pausing to look
at what he's remembered for most –

the Victoria Falls! Back to London he went,
to report on the sights that he'd seen.
He was feasted and fêted,
and funds were donated
to ship him straight back where he'd been.

His wife Mary decided to go with him too.
This time, David was told to explore
the River Zambezi,
which wasn't that easy,
what with rapids, and slavers galore.

---

2   Britain had been exporting opium to China from its poppy fields in
India. The Chinese were trying to end this trade.

Mary died of malaria, leaving him stunned.
The rest of them somehow survived.
Though his heart wasn't in it,
he did not for one minute
plan to stop, till a letter arrived

from London, which said that the plug had been pulled,
and he'd better return for a while.
So homeward he went,
and then back he was sent
to discover the source of the Nile!

He spent eight more years looking, but didn't succeed
(Lake Victoria's reckoned the source).
He had barely survived
when Stanley arrived
and said... but you know what, of course![3]

He'd been sent by his paper to find the great man,
and he brought him much-needed provisions.
'Come back home!' he implored,
advice David ignored –
not one of his wiser decisions,

for he died a year later, his search unfulfilled.
His servants expressed their devotion
(having buried his heart)
by proceeding to cart
his corpse to the Indian Ocean.

---

3   Henry Morton Stanley (1841–1904), correspondent of the
New York Herald, who is supposed to have said
'Doctor Livingstone, I presume?'

A RHYMING HISTORY

A ship brought him back, on his very last trip.
In the Abbey, he rests in the nave.
But perhaps he should lie
where he happened to die,
for that land was his life and his grave?

52.

FREDERICK SCOTT ARCHER

C. 1813 – 1 MAY 1857

Who gave 'wet-plate' photography to the world

Hands up, all those who know his name...
I thought so – one or two at most!
He didn't seem to covet fame.
Well, fair enough; but all the same,
he was a Great Brit, so he'll claim
a page or two to boast...

Stone-carving was his stock-in-trade –
memorials, and figures too.
But of the artefacts he made,
for which (one hopes) he was well-paid,
there's little record, I'm afraid –
are any left on view?

It's what he'd give, not what he'd sell,
that ought to make him famed today...
How could prospective buyers tell
if he could carve remotely well
when his delighted clientele
took all his work away?

Fred needed records, drawn by Light!
Fox Talbot's Calotypes, perhaps?[1]
This method, though, was sewn up tight,

---

1   William Henry Fox Talbot (1800–1877) improved on the
     Daguerreotype process.

and no non-payer had the right
to use it (though a legal fight
made Talbot's patent lapse).

The fee, we must assume, exceeded
what Frederick could safely spend.
So, nothing daunted, he proceeded
to buy the chemicals he needed
to find a new way, and succeeded!
His method marked the end

of Calotype supremacy,
for it was altogether better.
Its pictures had more clarity,
it had more sensitivity –
and it was absolutely free!
The Chemist got a letter

in which Fred set out to explain
the 'wet plate' process he'd devised.[2]
He forfeited all chance of gain –
it was in everyone's domain!
Had he been utterly insane?
What had his friends advised?

For twenty years, or even more,
it had world-wide success...
We see what Dickens (q.v.) saw;
here's Lincoln in the Civil War,
and Kaiser Wilhelm, then aged four
(or maybe even less)

---

2   Archer's process, which used a freshly-coated glass plate, was
     published in March 1851.

caught by Fred's silver iodide;
Livingstone (q.v.), I presume;
and Victor Hugo, who'd just died;
while Brunel (q.v.) stands beside
his new ship, waiting for the tide –
I'm running out of room!

Despite all this activity,
Fred died with nothing but his name.
His colleagues in Photography
collected for a bursary
to help his stricken family,
feeling a sense of shame...

To pay him homage, you must go
to where he lies in Kensal Green.[3]
But there's no stone or mark, to show
this Great Brit's place six feet below;
so how could anybody know
that he had ever been?[4]

---

3   Information for pilgrims: he is buried in grave 2263/120/RS.
4   The 150th anniversary of Archer's death passed without any of the
        British photographic institutions drawing public attention to it.

53

JOHN RUSKIN

8 FEBRUARY 1819 – 20 JANUARY 1900

Who urged a reappraisal of art and architecture

John Ruskin's stock fell pretty low
for slighting Michelangelo,
and neither did he help it rise
by praising Turner to the skies –
Turner (q.v.), that bête noire
of those who liked things as they are!
This young man's violent polemics
against the cosy academics
began when he was 24;
he started banging on their door
with *Modern Painters*. This, in short,[1]
is what our innovator thought:
the Artist, Subject, and Creation
should mingle in a celebration
of Oneness, so that Nature's soul
is celebrated in the whole!
This metaphysical orgasm
(which fuelled his iconoclasm)
most celebrated Masters lacked –
their landscape backgrounds were, in fact,
assorted props and nothing more!
These precepts guided what he saw
in architectural styles too.
Stone was supreme, in Ruskin's view,

---

1   He published four volumes of *Modern Painters* (1843–56). His most
       celebrated work is *The Stones of Venice*, published in three
       volumes (1851–53).

once Gothic's airy arabesque
subdued the rounded Romanesque;
it gives one a transcendent feeling
to gaze up at a vault (or ceiling);
and in its carvers' work, to see
their individuality!
With churches in a sorry state,
he was a leading advocate
of unobtrusive *conservation*,
scorning aggressive restoration
to re-invoke an age that's gone –
an argument that still goes on
(e.g. Stonehenge). His Gothic passion
restored it to the height of fashion –
arched windows challenged Georgian square,
and were inserted everywhere
in deference to public taste,
which naturally became debased –
'Mock-Gothic' is the term we use!
It's no surprise that Ruskin's views
on art and craft and self-expression
should make a powerful impression
on his devoted acolytes
(the self-styled Pre-Raphaelites)
who painted every leaf and flower
with almost microscopic power.
The drudgery of laissez-faire
drove Ruskin almost to despair...
how could his higher hopes succeed
when Labour was ground down by Greed?
His views on the Economy
matched William Morris's (q.v.),
who shared his mentor's view of Art
as Labour coming from the Heart.

54.

FLORENCE NIGHTINGALE

12 MAY 1820 – 13 AUGUST 1910

'The Lady with the Lamp'

Like Elizabeth Fry
(who's an earlier Great),
Florence thought: 'Why should I,
born to woman's estate,
be condemned and constrained
by Society's rules?
What shall I have gained
by suckling fools?'
Elizabeth, though,
was a mother by then,
whereas Florence said 'No'
to a bevy of men.
She in fact fell in love
with a writer of Verse,[1]
but a Voice from above
said her job was to nurse.
Mamma was appalled
at her daughter's request,
for nurses (so-called)
were mere drudges at best;
but her father had taught her
maths, science, and art,
and with funds to support her
she was able to start
on her spiritual mission

---

1   Richard Monckton Milnes, 1809–1885

after meeting (DV)
a renowned politician,
Sidney Herbert, MP.[2]

When Russia invaded
the Turkish dominion,
the government (aided
by public opinion)
sent our troops off to thwart
this aggressive idea
by seizing their port
in the southern Crimea,
called Sebastopol. Well,
The Times's reporter
had a story to tell
of the terrible slaughter
and the lack of provision
of medical care –
hence Flo's sudden decision
that she had to be there.
She told Sidney, her friend
(now of Cabinet rank),
who agreed in the end,
so it's him we must thank
for letting her go
to what's now Istanbul.
The sight appalled Flo!
The place was so full
that the soldiers were lying
unwashed on the floor,
untended and dying
as ships brought in more.
You didn't breathe air –

---

2   Sidney Herbert (1810–1861), was War Secretary during the
        Crimean conflict.

you breathed sewage instead
(which meant rats everywhere).
'I have never,' Flo said,
'endured such a smell.
How could you expect
the sick to get well?
Now, Sidney, I've checked
on the things that we'll need,
like blankets and soap
(all the rest you can read
in my list); and I hope
that the Catering Corps
(who supply what they eat)
will provide a lot more
healthy, nourishing *meat*!'
At his desk in Whitehall
Sidney felt under fire;
but that wasn't all –
indignation rose higher
when Flo leaked to the Press
the most newsworthy bits,
and the scandalous mess
made breakfasting Brits
(once she had got back)
support her position
when she launched an attack,
through a Royal Commission,
on the treatment provided
for the hospital cases.
Florence also decided
that there ought to be places
where women could train
to be qualified nurses,
and began a campaign
that unclasped enough purses
to start a Foundation

that bears her name still;[3]
a deserved celebration
of her God-given will.

For her last 15 years
Florence kept to her bed,
or so it appears
from what I have read.
It seems rather a shame
that her role was reversed;
but at least she could claim
she was properly nursed!

---

3   Now the Florence Nightingale School of Nursing and Midwifery, at
      King's College, London.

55.

WILLIAM BOOTH

10 APRIL 1829 – 20 AUGUST 1912

He and his wife Catherine founded the Salvation Army

He was more than a match for Bryant & May,
whose women were working a punishing day,
one shilling and fourpence their maximum pay,
and their faces were steadily rotting away.
Hard for them to acknowledge the Lord!

They dipped sticks into phosphorus, forming a head,
and that was the cause of the dying and dead,
since the chemical compound was yellow, not red.
The red sort was safe, but the management said
it cost more than the firm could afford.

So William established a rival concern,
paying twice what those ill-fated ladies could earn,
which proved that red phosphorus showed a return;
and he opened its doors so that others could learn
how to profit *and* honour the Lord...

William's pawnbroking background had made him aware
of the millions that lived on the brink of despair.
He heard God in his teens (as did others elsewhere),
and the gist of it was that he ought to prepare
the lapsed and the lost for the Lord.

He met Catherine Mumford, and married her too,
in spite of a major discordance of view
regarding what women should rightfully do.

She felt that the moment was long overdue
when her gender stood up for the Lord.

Five years later, in chapel, she rose in her place,
the sublimest sensation suffusing her face,
and spoke off the cuff with such consummate grace
that William acknowledged the strength of her case –
yes, women *could* speak for the Lord!

As a Methodist preacher he'd started his mission,
but their leaders disliked his hellfire tuition,
since the Bible he bashed threatened utter perdition
for those who refused to show heartfelt contrition,
or who questioned the Word of the Lord!

With music and singing and clapping en masse,
and with bread in the oven and soup on the gas,
he hoped to rekindle the Light; but alas,
their souls remained sunk in the social morass.
How could they acknowledge the Lord

when nothing got better, although they had prayed?
Without heavenly hopes, would they feel afraid
of the fires of Hell and the price to be paid?
Hence William and Catherine's social crusade –
an Army, with Jesus its sword![1]

He wrote *Darkest England*, with data to show[2]
that millions of people had fallen so low
they had no expectations, and nowhere to go –
which was not what the middle class wanted to know!
Their secular work struck a chord

---

1   Their movement started in East London, and was originally called
the Christian Mission (1865). It was re-christened the
Salvation Army in 1878.

2   *In Darkest England and the Way Out*, 1890

with social progressives, who broadly agreed
with offering shelter to people in need.
And the facts in his book were unpleasant indeed,
which made it a 'must' for reformers to read;
but Shaftesbury (q.v.) deplored

the gospel they preached, which was based upon fear.
And William's position was perfectly clear,
that the bread and the soup were to make it appear
that Jesus was smiling, and heaven was here –
if only they'd clap for the Lord!

But regardless of what its detractors may say,
the Army worked wonders at Bryant & May,
and looked after girls in the family way;
and its million-plus conscripts are fighting today
against misery here and abroad.

The number of souls that have met their Creator
thanks to William's good work, and his followers' later,
has not been released in its publicised data;
but the rate of Salvation is bound to be greater
with the Army proclaiming the Lord!

56.

WILLIAM MORRIS
24 MARCH 1834 – 3 OCTOBER 1896

Interior designer and Socialist

The name of William Morris brings to mind
leaves, stems and flowers, formally entwined,
with all the details exactly right –
he was, in other words, Pre-Raphaelite!
His art looked back to what he thought had been
a better age, pre-dating the Machine.
Using your hands, whatever you were making,
helped put your soul into the undertaking –
whether you fashioned all or just a part,
such work enriched, it was a form of Art.

In Medieval times, William professed,
Nature and Toil were at their happiest,
and based on this, in 1861,
an optimistic venture was begun:
Morris & Co's prospectus proudly speaks
of using pre-industrial techniques
for making Furnishings and Tableware –
come to our showrooms in Red Lion Square,
which also stock our Wallpapers, of course!
In all this, William was the driving force;
but later, having moved to Oxford Street
(the province, at that time, of the elite),
he worried that his business did so well
simply because his wealthy clientele
had made their pile from that rapacious evil
called mass-production – most un-Medieval!
Das Kapital, by Marx, had made him see
that to eliminate the bourgeoisie,
the workers of the country must resist,
so William now became a Socialist.
His meetings often landed him in court,
for in the eighties serious fights were fought
when out-of-workers marched, demanding power
(farmers were ruined by imported flour).
But basically he was bourgeois too –
how could he tell the Starving what to do
when his idea of gentle relaxation
was doing Homer in a new translation?[1]
(Some of my readers may not be aware
that he was shown the Poet Laureate's chair
when Tennyson died [q.v.]. But he declined.)
So, as I said, what brings his name to mind
is that unfading foliage of his,
which you can still obtain from Liberty's.

---

1   Morris' translation of the *Odyssey* was published in 1887.

57

ANDREW CARNEGIE

25 NOVEMBER 1835 – 11 AUGUST 1919

Who believed it was wrong to die rich

The power of Steam and Smoke combined
made Andrew's Dad despair...
Hand-weaving had been undermined –
they'd have to move elsewhere!

Farewell, Dunfermline! Set off west!
They sailed to the States,
where Andrew proved that he possessed
entrepreneurial traits.

He saw the future was in Steel,
and worked prodigiously...
He grew so rich that he could feel
(when he was 33):

'I've made more money than I need.
If my soul's to survive,
I must pause every day, and *read* –
then quit at 35!'

Despite this, he grew richer still,
accruing millions more,
thanks to his Pittsburgh steel mill
that processed iron ore

in unexampled quantities
to serve the growing trade.
More flowed out of his furnaces
than far-off Britain made!

His mill-hands worked for rotten pay
(ensuring his success);
but after their exhausting day
he planned, through his largesse

to benefit the labour force.
Books were, he thought, the key.
How to supply them, though? Of course –
a *public library*![1]

'The noblest use of wealth,' he stated,
'promotes the Arts and Learning.'
So to this end he dedicated
the millions he was earning.[2]

But not a penny would he give
where charity began.
Not welfare but *initiative*
impelled this self-made man!

'To die rich is to die disgraced,'
is what he liked to say.
Well, Andrew's honourably placed
through what he gave away!

---

1   He endowed 2,500 public libraries in the USA, Britain
     and elsewhere.
2   He put $350 million into Trusts for this purpose.

58.

JOSEPH ROWNTREE

24 MAY 1836 – 24 FEBRUARY 1925

Industrialist and philanthropist

This cocoa-maker
was a Quaker,
which seems to be the key
to his success
in Busy-ness
and his Philanthropy.

His father made
his name in Trade...
In York, when 21,
he'd bought a shop
and worked non-stop.
The empire had begun!

This shop of his
sold groceries;
but Joseph's brother thought
a better bet
was chocolate,
and so he went and bought

an enterprise
of modest size –
a dozen men would do
to pack the stuff.
They were enough
till Joseph joined him too...[1]

---

1   He joined his brother's firm in 1867.

He took on more,
and by '04
3,000-plus clocked in!
How could he please
his employees?
The first thing he'd begin

were Pensions, which
(now he was rich)
he funded from his wealth.
Then he began
a Widows' Plan;
a Doctor for their health;

with Cookery
compulsory
for maids not yet espoused;
but would he dare
to Profit-share?
Much aggro was aroused

by those who said
it would, instead,
assist the Bosses' ends;
because (of course)
the labour force
would boost *their* dividends![2]

But what about
all those Without?
Their plight seemed so unjust,
at his behest
a huge bequest
endowed the Rowntree Trust.

---

2   The shared-profits scheme was eventually adopted in 1923.

Is that the lot?
No, I forgot –
he built a vast estate
to house the Poor.[3]
I'm pretty sure
all this *must* make him Great!

---

3   This was his intention, but New Earswick ended up with mixed
housing – a 'model village'.

59

THOMAS HARDY

2 JUNE 1840 – 11 JANUARY 1928

Novelist, poet, and re-creator of Wessex

'When I set out for Lyonesse' (revised version)

When I set out for Lyonesse[1]
in 1868,
I reached a most attractive spot,
the parish of St Juliot.
Its church had started to decay,
and with the Rector I would stay
until the building had been checked
(I'd trained to be an architect).
I found the Rectory and knocked...
The door by Emma was unlocked.
Hers was the Hand of Fate!

When I came back from Lyonesse,
I was a different man.
We'd climbed the cliff above the sea,
her hair (as I wrote) flapping free,
her gown the colour of the air.
So we became a married pair...
Had we been blessed with tiny feet
they might have made our lives complete;
but things must be as they are willed.
My life (and hers) felt unfulfilled,
and separateness began.

---

1   'Lyonesse' is Hardy's romantic Arthurian (q.v.) name for Cornwall.

My books, though, were a great success.
Far From the Madding Crowd
(my fourth, in 1874)
pushed open the proverbial door.
I wrote of people, places, ways
remembered from my childhood days,
when through a Dorset now quite altered
my three-mile school-bound footsteps faltered.
The name of 'Wessex' I applied
to this memorial countryside –
and it has done me proud!

While she and I talked less and less,
the public fêted me.
I built Max Gate; behind its wall
we hardly spoke a word at all.
My last two novels (*Tess* and *Jude*)
were deemed offensive, if not rude –
surprisingly, my sales dropped,
and so my novel-writing stopped.
At this point I began again,
refilled my versatile pen,
and turned to poetry.

But I was stunned by my distress
when Emma passed away.
Her vanished presence seemed to free
the censorship of memory:
a little glass we'd left behind
when picnicking, now came to mind
four decades since we ate and drank
beside that sparkling river bank.
Poems began to pour like tears,
revisiting our sunless years –
the best I wrote, some say![2]

---

2   'Poems of 1912–1913' published in *Satires of Circumstance*, 1914

I once returned to Lyonesse,
where Fate first played its part.
I should be grateful, I suppose;
it could have been much worse, God knows.
I lord the literary scene –
but oh, how lonely I have been!
They've hatched a plan to bury me
in Poet's Corner. Well, we'll see
(at least you will) – but kindly save
a souvenir for Emma's grave,
and let her share my heart.[3]

---

[3]   Hardy was buried in Westminster Abbey, but his heart was interred, at his request, in Emma's grave at Stinsford Church, Dorset.

60.

DR THOMAS JOHN BARNARDO
4 JULY 1845 – 19 SEPTEMBER 1905

An evangelising social worker

When Tom was a child
he was headstrong and wild,
but at 16 God showed him the Light,
and said to him 'Please
convert the Chinese.'
So Tom pondered, and answered: 'All right!'

A RHYMING HISTORY

Learning medicine, he felt,
was a must; so he dwelt
in London's East End while he trained.
But the children he found
with no bed but the ground
made him wonder how much would be gained

by going out there
when these waifs needed prayer,
shelter, hygiene, and balanced nutrition.
There was heaps to do here –
that was only too clear.
Helping young Brits in need was his mission!

Tom networked like mad
through the contacts he had,
and Lord Shaftesbury helped him (q.v.).
Empty houses were leased,
and this doctor-cum-priest
filled them up with his human debris.

His wife Syrie took part
in the work from the start,
and a Village for Girls was their dream.
They managed it, too –
a community grew
with a thousand or more in the scheme.

But as well as repair,
Tom was also aware
that his charges would need a vocation.
Restored and equipped,
18,000 were shipped
to new lands through *enforced emigration*.

No heroic scheme grows
without treading on toes;
was he right to snatch children away
from their own flesh and blood
if they're covered in mud?
Well, I leave that for others to say!

61

ALEXANDER GRAHAM BELL

3 MARCH 1847 – 2 AUGUST 1922

Inventor of the telephone and many other things

'Mr Watson, come here please – I want you!' he said,
in March 1876.
But Bell's order came via
an electrical wire,
and instead of a series of clicks

which the telegraph made when a message was sent,
Mr Watson could hear every word
telephonically –
and this turned out to be
the first non-human voice ever heard!

Bell's business was words, for this hard-working Scot
had a father (and grandfather too)
who had studied the way
people speak what they say –
which is what he decided to do.

In due course, the family sailed off west.
In Boston, our pioneer taught
the Deaf elocution
at the first Institution
that was founded for work of this sort.[1]

---

1   Sarah Fuller's School for the Deaf. Incidentally, he married one of
his pupils, Mabel Hubbard.

He examined the organ of hearing, to learn
how the sound it receives is converted
by the drum in the ear
into words we can hear.
But at this point, his thoughts were diverted

by the thought that a membrane, if made to respond
to the sound waves a speaker emitted,
could by its vibrations
cause electric pulsations.
And then, if a wire transmitted

these pulses to some other membrane elsewhere,
it would speak the original sound.
So why write a letter?
It would be a lot better
to have *telephones* scattered around!

A thin steel disc was Bell's clever solution.
Due to Faraday's findings (q.v.),
its vibrations produced
a current, induced
electromagnetically.

His patent was stamped and protected in law;
three days later, those first words were spoken.[2]
Competitors fought
his invention in court,
but his rightful claim couldn't be broken.

Thomas Edison soon turned his mind to it too,
and came up with the *carbon transmitter*,[3]
which worked ten times as well
as the one used by Bell.
Their feud grew exceedingly bitter,

---

2   His telephone patent was approved on 7 March 1876; the first words
were transmitted on the tenth.

3   Thomas Edison (1847–1931) discovered that carbon granules make a
better microphone than Bell's metal diaphragm.

but agreement was reached, and he earned a lot more
from the royalty fees he was paid.
Then he turned his attention
to another invention –
recording what's said or what's played![4]

Hence the *Gramophone*, also of social import,
for a set of recordings would mean
that music could play
in one's house night and day
(as long as you wound the machine).

Bell devised an electrical way to locate
the bullet, when someone was shot.
And what about kites
that flew men to great heights?
And the flaps that all aircraft have got

at the back of the wing, to help them take off,
and to alter their height as they go?
So when the phone rings,
reflect on these things,
and don't simply mutter 'Hallo?'

---

4   Edison took out the first 'phonograph' patent in 1878, but Alexander
     and his cousin Chichester Bell worked on the greatly
     improved 'graphophone'.

62.

SIR JOHN AMBROSE FLEMING
29 NOVEMBER 1849 – 18 APRIL 1945

Who made the first electronic valve

John Ambrose was a real Whizz
at Electricity.
The credit's very largely his
for generating quantities
of kilowatts from batteries
that flashed Marconi's messages[1]
(not always audibly)

from Cornwall to his distant crew
on Nova Scotia's heights.
And Edison employed him too
when incandescent lamps were new,[2]
and cities here were asking: 'Who
can tell us what we ought to do
to brighten up our nights?'

John founded an Electric Chair
(a professorial seat)
at UCL; and then and there[3]
he sat in it, and that is where
the eager students in his care
were introduced to the ampere
and other terms they'd meet.

---

1   Guglielmo Marconi (1874–1937) made the first confirmed
     transatlantic radio contact in December 1902.
2   Thomas Edison (1847–1931) invented the incandescent lamp in 1879.
3   He was Professor of Electrical Engineering at University College,
     London, 1885–1926.

John Ambrose held, for 40 years,
the highest of positions
among his fellow-pioneers.
A new technology appears,
with *electronic engineers*
clutching their headphones to their ears
while searching for transmissions!

To John Ambrose's valve we owe
the electronic age.
A filament *in vacuo*,
when heated up to make it glow
emits electrons (as you know),
which means a current starts to flow.
So he had set the stage

for Lee de Forest's adaptation[4]
(the *triode* valve) – the key
to feasible communication,
since it produced *amplification*.
John Ambrose started litigation
to make a case for compensation –
he lost, expensively!

In Sidmouth, I remember spying
a plaque on the address
where he had lived when he was dying.
Perhaps his ghost still walks there, sighing:
'If only I had thought of trying
the *triode* – there'd be no denying
I'd been a great success!'

---

4   The American, Lee de Forest (1873–1961) patented his triode valve,
       called the Audion, in 1908. Fleming had patented his 'diode'
       valve in November 1904.

63.

HORATIO HERBERT, LORD KITCHENER

24 JUNE 1850 – 5 JUNE 1916

'The People's Soldier'

'Your Country Needs YOU!' That's the way
Lord Kitchener's recalled today.
On every wall in every road
that famous face, moustachio'd,
made millions sign and join the cause
and fight the war to end all wars;
and now, engraved in stone instead,
we read their names among the dead.

But he was famous long before
the carnage of the First World War –
by then, he was a Grand Old Man!
He'd led our force in the Sudan
against those in the population
unhappy with our occupation,
which evidently lacked finesse.
Once he had sorted out the mess
(we're back in 1898)
he started to Administrate,
which was, as far as I can tell,
what Kitchener did very well.
He had the mosques we'd damaged mended;
their holy Friday he defended,
and evangelicals were banned
from trying to Christianise the land.

Then to South Africa, to meet
the Boers, whom he duly beat;
he wanted them to have a share
of the immense resources there,
but Britain balked, and left unsigned
the treaty that he had in mind.
So Kitchener now had to face
an armed and hostile populace;
suspects were herded up and shot,
or put in camps and left to rot.
(The treaty to conclude the war
resembled what he'd urged before.)

The Great War brought an urgent call
for Kitchener to help Whitehall.
Unlike his colleagues, he foresaw
no early ending to the war –
without a huge recruitment drive
it was unlikely we'd survive.
His poster was his big success;
munitions were a dreadful mess,
and Winston Churchill's plan (q.v.)
to occupy Gallipoli,
when thousands died in the attack
earned Kitchener a lot of flak
for sending too few men too late.
But did he earn his watery fate
when mines laid by a submarine
sank him, in June 1916?
To fight the fight that lay ahead
he'd still recruit, though he was dead.

64

CECIL JOHN RHODES

5 JULY 1853 – 26 MARCH 1902

Imperialist and exploiter

Of all my Britons, I suspect,
he's *least* politically correct;
but though his reputation's dark,
he staked his claim and left his mark.
His view was, in a nutshell, thus:
'The whole world should be ruled by us!'
Sent out there to improve his health,
South Africa's potential wealth
turned Rhodes into a buccaneer.
A speculator named de Beer
had bought a diamond concession;
the shares fell during a depression,
so Rhodes and his companion Rudd[1]
invested in its bluish mud,
which, having spewed forth gem on gem,
made millionaires of both of them.
The Brits had been extremely keen
to snatch these regions for the Queen –
the Boers (Dutch) got there before,
and we'd already fought one war.
Now came the ill-starred Jameson Raid,
when Rhodes's heavily-armed brigade
marched on Johannesburg – he planned
to free the region (called the Rand)
from Boer control. This came to naught,

---

1   Charles Dunnell Rudd (1844–1916)

but it was generally thought
to be a British-backed campaign –
so we were soon at war again!
A few years later, Rhodes was dead.
A Will that he had drafted, said
that his vast fortune should be spent
on aggrandizing the extent
of British Rule (he itemised
the countries to be colonised).
Well, these demands were pretty tough,
and since there wasn't quite enough,
it went into a fund, to pay
for scholars from the USA,
or Germany, or foreign lands
that once had been in British hands,
to go to Oxford, in his name.[2]
So anyone who's had a claim
on one of Rhodes's bursaries
will overlook these quirks of his.

---

2   About 90 Rhodes Scholarships are awarded annually, including 32
         for students from the USA.

65.

ROBERT STEPHENSON SMYTH, LORD BADEN-POWELL

22 FEBRUARY 1857 – 8 JANUARY 1941

Who founded the Scout movement

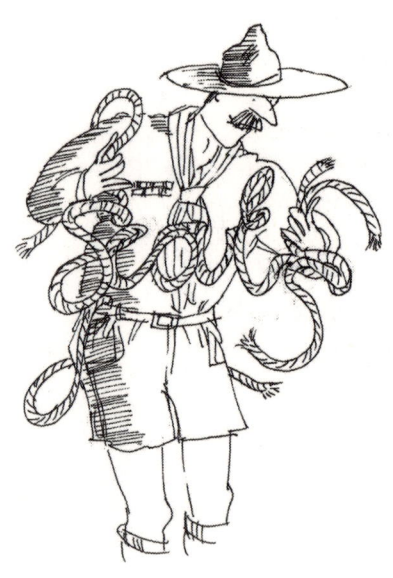

'Man, Nation, Maiden
Please call it Baden.
Further, for Powell
Rhyme it with Noel.'
So now you all know
that it's not 'Pow' but 'Po'
(those lines are a quote

from something he wrote).
B-P, as he's known,
began on his own
the organisation
that dazzled the nation
and met boys' desires
to sit around fires
and sleep out of doors,
taking turns with the chores.
Since girls couldn't scout
they were feeling left out,
but the Guides soon began,
which his sister first ran
(until Olave, his wife,
became Chief Guide for life),
and now Guiding and Scouting
were the ultimate outing!
But what of B-P?
Here's a compact CV...
The South African wars
were the principal cause
of the Movement he founded;
being really well grounded
in the ways of the wild
since he'd camped as a child,
he was used as a scout.
The amount he found out
caused no end of surprise;
with his network of spies
he kept hiding and seeking
till besieged in Mafeking
by a Boer formation
whose aim was starvation,
since our force wasn't large.
As the Colonel-in-Charge,
B-P made their stocks last

while two hundred days passed
till the town was relieved.[1]
The acclaim he received
meant further promotion –
but he soon had the notion
that boys might have fun
doing things he had done,
so he wrote them all out,
and became their Chief Scout!

---

1   16 May 1900

66

SIR EDWARD WILLIAM ELGAR

2 JUNE 1857 – 23 FEBRUARY 1934

Who wrote two ever-popular compositions

I must confess, I'm not quite clear
why Edward Elgar should be here
and not Vaughan Williams, Holst, or Britten,
considering the amount they'd written;
but he outpolled the other three
when canvassed by the BBC.[1]
His major works are rather few;
he wrote a symphony or two,
a cello piece (which in her day
inspired Jacqueline du Pré),[2]
much choral music, and of course
that oratoric tour-de-force
about Gerontius' Dream.[3]
But Elgar's popular esteem
rests on two long-enduring hits
that stake his claim among these Brits.
First, the 'Enigma Variations',
his musical impersonations
of 14 people in his life.
The first one represents his wife,
the last is of himself; but who
comes thirteenth? Elgar left no clue!
They were an overnight success,

---

1   He came sixtieth in the BBC poll of Top Britons, 2002.
2   The noted cellist (1945–1987)
3   'The Dream of Gerontius', a two-part oratorio (1900)

entered the nation's consciousness,
and must have helped his great commission –
a brave and martial composition
to sound the spirit of the Nation
at Edward's heady coronation,
after Victoria's age had passed.
Hence 'Pomp and Circumstance' – a blast
of molten brass and screaming choir,
their passion rising ever higher
as flag-wrapped Prommers give their all
within the heaving Albert Hall,
and everybody there behaves
as though the Brits still rule the waves.
But Elgar's spirit isn't here –
it's in his native Worcestershire,
where he would go out for a hike
or ride his solid-tyre bike,
hearing the music in the air
to re-create for us to share.

67.

EMMELINE PANKHURST

14 JULY 1858 – 14 JUNE 1928

A prominent member of the Suffragette Movement

Emmeline Pankhurst and her daughters[1]
(flanked by their militant supporters)
considered words as wasted air
that wouldn't get them anywhere.
Why couldn't other women see
that in a true democracy
they ought to be enfranchised too?

---

1   Her two most active daughters were Christabel Harriette
      (1880–1958) and Estelle Sylvia (1882–1960).

They formed the WSPU;[2]
its slogan 'Deeds Not Words' excused
the methods that its members used –
volleying bricks through window panes
or padlocking themselves with chains
or breaking meetings up; in short,
its membership appeared in court
as often as the law allowed,
refusing (cheered on by the crowd)
to pay the fine or meet the bail,
which meant they had to go to gaol,
where they refused all prison food.
Force-feeding changed the public mood;
this most distasteful way of dining
meant sentiment began inclining
towards these quasi-martyrs' Cause,
when breaking windows, heads, and laws
had not. The government rushed through
the 'Cat and Mouse' Bill... What they'd do[3]
is set the hunger-strikers free,
let them regain vitality,
and then return them to their cell
as soon as they were fit and well.
Despite all this, it was the War,
not hunger strikes, that changed the law,
since Emmeline had thought it wiser
to turn her girls against the Kaiser.
The slogan now became 'Recruit!'
A male in a civilian suit
accosted by her fervent crew
would soon learn what he ought to do –
his proper place was in the trenches,
letting her women man the benches,

---

2   Women's Social and Political Union, founded 1903
3   The Prisoners (Temporary Discharge for Ill Health) Act, 1913

producing powder, shell and shot
(of which the men used quite a lot).
Before the War had run its course,
the women's growing labour force
ensured a measure of consent
to female enfranchisement.
They got the Vote at 30 then,
reduced to 21 (like men)
in the year 1928;
though, sadly, this came just too late
for Emmeline, who'd gone to rest
where nothing moves her to protest.

68.

ALFRED CHARLES WILLIAM HARMSWORTH (LORD NORTHCLIFFE)

15 JULY 1865 – 14 AUGUST 1922

The founder of 'popular' journalism

A journalist he started out,
a journalist he stayed.
He never had the slightest doubt
that money could be made

if he could feed the public taste
and make them pay for more!
On this premise his plans were based.
In 1894

The Evening News faced bankruptcy.
He got the backing needed,
took over editorially,
and brilliantly succeeded!

His titles were more titillating;
the pictures were a plus;
the text was less intimidating
(though pretty dense to us!).

Harmsworth, with all these points in mind,
then launched the *Daily Mail*,[1]
so innovatively designed
that when it went on sale

---

1   The *Daily Mail* was launched on 4 May 1896.

he knew he had produced a winner.
It was a revelation!
Sport, gossip, what to cook for dinner;
a serialisation...

The *Daily Mail* broke the mould.
As Harmsworth had supposed,
it wasn't just the news that sold.
In due course he proposed

a newspaper for women, called
the *Daily Mirror*. Well,
he launched the thing, then watched appalled
as sales fell and fell![2]

To try to recoup what he'd lost
meant major alterations.
He cut the text and halved the cost,
and upped the illustrations,

and sales soared with less to read!
Soon, Harmsworth was aware
that other newspapers might need
his tender loving care...

The Times was in a parlous way,
and *The Observer* too.
He bought them both, and made them pay.
The knighthood he was due

he put off, saying he would wait
until a peerage came.
And so, when only 38,
'Lord Northcliffe' got his name!

---

2   The *Daily Mirror* was launched on 2 Nov 1903, with a female
       editorial staff.

His influence, as you'll have guessed,
grew uncontrollably.
To governments he was a pest.
Lord Kitchener (q.v.)

was mercilessly criticised
as millions broke their fast.
When K's torpedoed boat capsized,
his scribes proclaimed 'At last!'

The scandal over faulty shells
made appetising reading;
disaster at the Dardanelles
just couldn't help succeeding

in boosting circulation too!
Lloyd George, in desperation,[3]
gave him a Whitehall job to do,
in charge of Information.

Though Northcliffe's influence declined,
the *Mirror* and the *Mail*
preserve the tenets he defined
when they first went on sale...

---

3   David Lloyd George (1863–1945) became prime
        minister of the coalition government in December 1916.

69.

ROBERT FALCON SCOTT
6 JUNE 1868 – 29 MARCH 1912

Who reached the South Pole too late

The final words of Lawrence Oates[1]
form one of those enduring quotes
that seem to make defeat success
(his name would be recalled much less
if he had lived instead of died).
He said to Scott: 'I'm off outside –
I may be some time.' Out he went,
and left the others in the tent...

Scott's South Pole exploits had begun
when he went in 1901
aboard the ship *Discovery*.
With Ernest Shackleton (q.v.)
and Edward Wilson, they progressed
much further than the previous best,
but didn't make it all the way.
Years of frustration and delay
meant waiting until 1910
before he could depart again
(once all the fundraising was over)
aboard the good ship *Terra Nova*.

Roald Amundsen had left too,[2]
exactly the same aim in view,

---

1   It was Captain Oates' thirty-second birthday.
2   Roald Amundsen (1872–1928), the Norwegian explorer who reached
        the South Pole on 14 December 1911.

aboard the *Fram*, designed for ice –
which, crushing like a giant vice,
could make Scott's ship a total wreck.
The Brits thus had a longer trek
once all their gear was disembarked;
and money had been earmarked
for scientific observations
from specially-selected stations –
the Pole was not the only prize
(apart from in Joe Public's eyes!)
Before they'd even left, Scott reckoned
that they would probably be second;
but when they reached the Pole, and found
Amundsen's litter left around,
how bitter must have been the taste![3]
Then, battling through the howling waste
to get back to a food supply,
the five of them began to die...

The first one, Edgar Evans, fell;
he had no hope of getting well,
and very soon his wits had gone.
The next was Oates, who'd struggled on –
one foot was useless, killed by frost,
which slowed them all, at fatal cost,
for even though he 'went outside'
they reached a standstill, froze, and died.
Six months their tent remained their tomb;
Scott's journal, which foresaw their doom,
brought them the fame that they deserved
when he was found, quite well preserved,
with Wilson (from their earlier trip)
and Henry Bowers. His leadership
was questioned, maybe rightly so;
but their heroics in the snow
lent far more glory to those five
than if they'd all come back alive.

---

3   They reached the South Pole on 17 January 1912.

70.

SIR EDWIN LANDSEER LUTYENS

29 MARCH 1869 – 1 JANUARY 1944

The best-known architect of the twentieth century?

'*Ned Lutyens* great?' I hear you laugh.
'He built New Delhi – true.
But surely it's the Cenotaph
to which his fame is due?'

Reader, this vigorous riposte
(for which you're not to blame)
suggests my case is far from lost –
it proves you know his name!

Since Nash, no one I can recall
has earned such admiration.
Whose hand designed the Albert Hall?
Earls Court? St Pancras Station?

The London Eye? The Modern Tate?
The National Theatre? [1]
They may all qualify as Great –
but Ned is known much better!

His illness as a youth stopped Ned
from taking a degree.
This may have been, he later said,
why architecturally

---

1   I leave you to look these up.

he started off with brick and stone
used in traditional ways.
Walking the Surrey lanes alone,
on cottages he'd gaze

and workmen building them as well.
This county was, he felt,
the place to find his clientele –
the new commuter belt!

When Gertrude Jekyll bought a plot
and built a residence
to Ned's design, he learned a lot
from her holistic sense.[2]

The gardens she designed, expressed
abundant energy.
The house (this was the acid test)
should settle seamlessly

into its garden, and appear
part of the landscape too!
During this phase of his career
Ned's reputation grew

until his enterprise had gained
a dominant position.
Among the contracts he obtained
was an immense commission

to plan New Delhi, and create
the Viceroy's palace there –
effectively a walled estate
a kilometre square![3]

---

2   Gertrude Jekyll (1843–1932) the most influential garden designer of
        her time. Her name rhymes with treacle.

3   The work on New Delhi (among many other jobs) occupied
        Lutyens from 1912 until 1929.

A RHYMING HISTORY

It has a classical façade,
a far-from-English dome;
Ned once again was trying hard
(as with a Surrey home)

to make a pleasing synthesis –
in this case, east and west.
Soon after he had started this
he answered a request

to raise a monument to those
who'd fallen in the War.[4]
The upshot everybody knows –
it's what he's famous for.

No edge is straight, no angle Right;
the Cenotaph's designed
to seem what it is not, despite
what goes on in the mind.

Even in minor instances
Ned's thoughtfulness is found.
That's why a nursery of his
has windows near the ground!

---

4   The Cenotaph was completed in 1920; a temporary one was rushed
     up in 1919 for the post-war Victory Parade.

71.

BERTRAND ARTHUR WILLIAM, LORD RUSSELL

18 MAY 1872 – 2 FEBRUARY 1970

Philosopher, writer and broadcaster

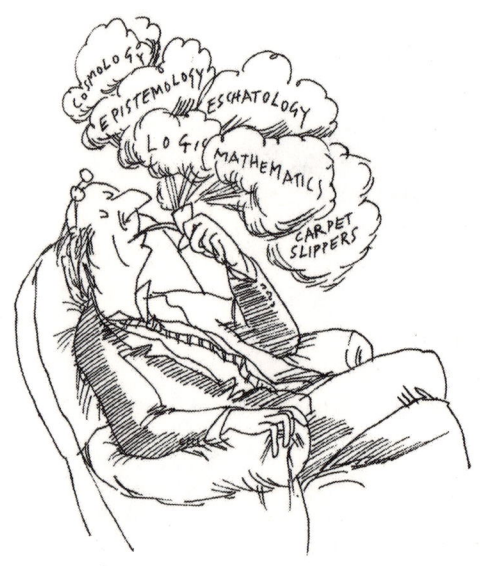

At 87, Bertrand Russell
added his philosophic muscle
to CND's impassioned cause[1]
to Ban the Bomb from future wars.
We saw his famous head of hair,

---

1   Campaign for Nuclear Disarmament, founded 1958

190

the focus of Trafalgar Square,
explaining to the reverent throng
why weapons of this type are wrong –
why Britain ought to shame the rest
and dump the warheads she possessed.
This brilliant and world-famous man
was so committed to a Ban
that he resigned from the Campaign,
convinced that talking was in vain,
and joined a hundred well-known names[2]
determined to promote their aims
through *civil disobedience.*
Having incited this offence,
our hero (88) was sent
to Brixton Prison, to repent.

I've started near the end, because
I'm not quite sure what Russell *was.*
He did, as far as I can see,
great favours for Philosophy
as a result of his decision
that words need mathematical precision
if they're to be of any use.
His arguments are so abstruse
they baffle simple brains like mine;
but he encouraged Wittgenstein,
who said (I think I've got it right)
that words are never watertight.
This sort of stuff would hardly seem
to earn much popular esteem,
but Russell's gift for thinking clearly
on every subject (very nearly)
and letting people share his thoughts,
made him a superstar of sorts,

---

2   The Committee of 100, founded 1960

and this (as well as dotting 'i's)
was worthy of the Nobel Prize.
His voice was principally heard
in thoughtful programmes on the Third,[3]
so when he stood up in the Square
with newspapers and TV there,
he was, as you'd expect, a Hit!
(That's why this poem starts with it.)

---

3   The Third Programme, forerunner of Radio 3

72.

SIR ERNEST
HENRY SHACKLETON

15 FEBRUARY 1874 – 5 JANUARY 1922

Antarctic explorer

The dreadful weather took its toll,
but Robert Falcon Scott
did get to the Antarctic Pole,
which Shackleton did not.

Ernest was in the first attack
that Scott had led (q.v.).
Their food ran out, so he came back
and married Emily.

A few years passed away, and then
the Pole's untrodden snow
made Ernest yearn to find some men
and have another go!

He fund-raised, bought a ship, made plans...
The *Nimrod* expedition
got his exhausted team to man's
most southerly position![1]

King Edward thought this pretty good –
he had the hero knighted.
For three years Ernest's record stood,
until the Pole was sighted

---

1   They reached 88° 23' S (160 km from the Pole) on 9 January 1909.

by Amundsen, and then by Scott.[2]
Undaunted, Ernest planned
to raise more funds (he'd need a lot)
and *cross* this snowy land!

Endurance took them to the start;
but they had not yet landed
before the pack-ice broke apart
and crushed it. They were stranded!

Three little boats, 28 crew –
things didn't look too good.
So off went Ernest with a few
to get what help they could.

More than four months the stranded men
had managed to survive,
before the Boss appeared again
and brought them home alive!

The polar plateau called once more,
and once more he went back
to circumnavigate its shore,
but had a heart attack.

He would have been returned to her,
but Emily said 'No!
I'm sure my Ernest would prefer
to lie beneath the snow.'[3]

---

2   Roald Amundsen reached the Pole on 14 December 1911, Scott on
       17 January 1912.

3   Shackleton was buried at Grytviken, South Georgia.

73.

SIR WINSTON SPENCER CHURCHILL

30 NOVEMBER 1874 – 24 JANUARY 1965

Who became prime minister in May 1940, and rallied the nation during the darkest days of World War Two

He smoked, he drank, he stayed up far too late.
Despite these faults, he is our Greatest Great![1]

---

1   Churchill was voted No. 1 Brit in the 2002 BBC poll.

74.

WILLIAM RICHARD MORRIS (LORD NUFFIELD)

10 OCTOBER 1877 – 22 AUGUST 1963

Pioneer of mass production, and philanthropist

Lord Nuffield! I was amazed
that when the BBC appraised
the 100 Brits of greatest note
(based on a television vote)
you didn't figure in the list
as Tycoon and Philanthropist!
In Oxford, in your middle teens,
you mended self-propelled machines
which town and gown alike would bring
if something stopped their pedalling
(the solid tyres used at first
felt every stone, but did not burst).
Then, thinking some of them might like
a more up-market *motorbike*,
you fixed an engine to the frame,
and in a twinkling it became
a Morris Motor Cycle! Well,
it wasn't difficult to tell
that this line wouldn't take you far;
the horseless carriage (or the 'car')
was what the better-off were buying,
so making them was well worth trying.
With this growth industry in mind,
by 1912 you had designed
the 'Bull-Nosed' Morris (seating two –

that's all that most cars then could do);
production stopped during the War,
but then the 'Oxford', holding four
(thus suitable for family use),
appeared the year after the truce.
It sold so well that soon you felt
the need for a conveyor belt,
with workers working really fast
as bits of car went inching past.
Ford used this for his Model T –[1]
it greatly helped efficiency,
and did so when you tried it here:
at Cowley, in one hectic year,
56,000 cars were made!
But from the profits of your trade,
Oxford would reap the benefit –
a College (which cost quite a bit),[2]
four Chairs plus numerous donations,
and that most princely of Foundations
(named after you), which would begin
to fund research in medicine
and social care. It's estimated
that altogether you donated
well over thirty million quid
from what you made from what you did
to causes that ennoble you.
Your business merged in '52
with Austin; and in '68
was lost in the conglomerate
called British Leyland – RIP...
But thanks to your philanthropy,
the name of Morris will live on
long after all the oil's gone!

---

1   Henry Ford (1863–1947) started a moving assembly line in 1913.
2   He laid the foundation stone of Nuffield College in 1949.

75.

MARIE STOPES

15 OCTOBER 1880 – 2 OCTOBER 1958

A fighter for women's rights

Those early fights
for women's rights
inspired young Marie.
No suffragette
you ever met
was more concerned than she!

She wrote a book[1]
that shouted: 'Look!
Our husbands underrate us!
There's got to be
equality –
insist on equal status!'

Word got about –
the book sold out!
But in the USA,
when it was brought
before a court,
they banned it straight away.

Their law was tough
on 'women's stuff'.
Marie met Margaret Sanger,[2]
who thought as she,
but had to flee
for causing so much anger.

Margaret had taught
that women ought
to have the right to plan.
Their pregnancy
should not just be
dependent on the man!

But even here
it wasn't clear
how far Marie could go.
Should you obstruct
while being f★★★★d?
The Church, for one, said No![3]

---

1   *Married Love*, 1918
2   Margaret Higgins Sanger (1879–1966) fled to England from the USA
      in 1914.
3   The Church of England did not officially accept artificial methods of
      birth control until the Lambeth Conference of 1931.

She thought you should.
Wise Parenthood[4]
(her key to married bliss)
explored the ways –
which, in those days,
were rather hit-and-miss.

Some had high hopes
to get Ms Stopes
put under lock and key.
But she'd refuse
to change her views.
The rest is history!

She fought more fights
for women's rights –
e.g. jobs and taxation.
But all the same,
we link her name
with planning procreation...

---

4   Published in 1918

76.

SIR ALEXANDER FLEMING

6 AUGUST 1881 – 11 MARCH 1955

Who pioneered antibiotics, and discovered penicillin

When serving in the First World War,
the cases Captain Fleming saw
convinced him that we slaughtered more
by treating injuries
with *antiseptics*, which were then
employed to kill the pathogen
before it killed these wretched men.
This novel view of his

was based upon the supposition
that bodies were their own physician.
They fought a threatening condition
(like being wounded, say)
with their home-made bactericide,
which antiseptics nullified.
That's why so many patients died –
so he thought, anyway.

St Mary's, off the Edgware Road,
is where his patient research showed
(using glass vessels he had blowed –
a wonderful collection
requiring a lot of puff),
that egg-white, tears, and suchlike stuff
contains this chemical – enough
to fight against infection!

He called the substance 'lysozyme',
though such a notion didn't chime
with viewpoints current at the time
(it's 1922).
But then, in 1928,
he noticed a discarded plate
infected with a mould that ate
bacteria! He grew

a culture, by extracting some –
a type of *penicillium*;
so 'penicillin' would become
the name upon the label.
But even though he tried and tried
to get the essence purified
(or else it couldn't be applied),
he found it too unstable.

Floored by his lack of expertise,
Fleming's response was: 'Help me, please!'
One of our Jewish refugees
(with Hitler on the rise)
named Ernest Chain, joined Howard Florey[1]
in writing penicillin's story.
The three men rightly shared the glory –
also the Nobel Prize!

Had Fleming's lab been squeaky-clean,
the mould might never have been seen,
which, on the face of it, must mean
that millions (at a guess)
would be condemned to pine and die.
You might decide it's worth a try
to give this as the reason why
you live in such a mess!

---

1   Ernst Boris Chain (1906–1979), German biochemist; Howard Walter
      Florey (1898–1968), Australian pharmacologist. The Prize was
      awarded to all three in 1945.

77.

BERNARD LAW MONTGOMERY (LORD MONTGOMERY OF ALAMEIN)

17 NOVEMBER 1887 – 24 MARCH 1976

Victor of the Battle of Alamein, 1942

Montgomery, I fear, was not
a person you'd have liked a lot,
though those who soldiered at his side
would look upon their feats with pride.
Since World War One, he'd ruminated
on how fights should be orchestrated,
producing manuals explaining
the paramount effect of *training*.
He was a real fitness freak –
his own Division, once a week,
was sent off running (in his case
he did the route at walking pace).
Herr Hitler duly started arming...
The Army's state was so alarming
that Monty felt obliged to say
they should be doing things his way,
with noticeable lack of tact –
persuasion was a skill he lacked.
His methods, though, were shown to work
during the chaos of Dunkirk,
when, cool of head and clear of brain,
be brought his soldiers back again.
Then followed two long years of waiting –
for Monty, they were most frustrating.

The war, by 1942,
was being fought (in Stalin's view)
by Russia, while the Brits applauded!
North Africa alone afforded
a chance of military success;
Eighth Army, though, was in a mess,
and Rommel, in flamboyant style,
was chasing us towards the Nile.
But even so, Churchill (q.v.)
wouldn't appoint Montgomery,
the likeliest man to stop the rot;
instead, he sent for General Gott,
whose plane was downed by numerous hits
from eager folk in Messerschmitts,
whose action, viewed with hindsight, may
have swung the conflict Britain's way,
for Monty took Gott's empty place
and fashioned triumph from disgrace.
At Alam Halfa, he dug in –[1]
when Rommel found he couldn't win,
he had no option but to wait
till Monty broke the stalemate.
At Alamein, his finest hour,[2]
with overwhelming firepower
he pulverised his mighty foe,
who realised it was time to go.
Up Italy he fought his way
in concert with the USA
(he thought them amateur, and said
exactly what was in his head);
then D-Day came, and it was he
who bore the brunt of Normandy,
withstanding the all-out attack

---

1   31 August–4 September 1942
2   23 October–4 November 1942

which Hitler hoped would drive us back.
When peace came, Monty lost his role;
he was avoided, on the whole,
by those who'd needed him before –
but he *began* to win the war!

78.

JOHN LOGIE BAIRD

13 AUGUST 1888 – 14 JUNE 1946

Inventor of the first workable television system

John Logie Baird
was never scared
of trying something new.
One brainwave which
might make him rich
(a new air-cushioned shoe)

kept going flat,
so that was that!
But he proved, nevertheless,

that one could see
(though fuzzily)
by using *wireless*.

A disc prepared
by Logie Baird
had holes in it, and spun.
Each hole let through
part of the view,
which built up, one by one,

a crude mosaic.
Each piece would make
a photocell emit
an amp or watt,
until he'd got
(by using every bit)

an image, seen
upon a screen
however far away!
It was, I've heard,
extremely blurred,
compared with those today;

but he had proved
that when things moved,
their image did; and so
in '26
his box of tricks
was put on public show.[1]

---

1   The demonstration at Frith Street in London on 26 January 1926 was
witnessed by a number of scientists and a reporter for *The Times*.

His company
(BTDC)[2]
broadcast the Derby live
in '31,
but had begun
to lose, by '35

its leading place.
It lost the race
since EMI could start[3]
making a set
(the clearest yet)
with not one moving part.

It's like the kind
that you would find
before the plasma screen.
(Well, more or less!)
So you can guess
what that was going to mean

for Baird's invention.
But let me mention
some other things he tried.
He had a go
at *video*;
and though it's been denied,

it's fairly clear
that one idea
envisaged *radar* too,
ten years or more
before the War.
One more thing he would do,

---

2   The Baird Television Development Company was formed in 1927.
3   EMI had developed a 405-line picture. The best definition Baird
        could achieve was 240 lines.

or so it's said,
used infra-red
(which we give out at night)
to pave the way
for what today
bathes trespassers in light!

79.

THOMAS STEARNS 'T. S.' ELIOT

26 SEPTEMBER 1888 – 4 JANUARY 1965

The most influential poet of the twentieth century

Of T. S. Eliot it may be said,
he's greatly praised, but not so greatly read.
(He's an adopted Brit, I ought to say,
who came here from Missouri, USA.)
We're in the province of the literati;
mere humans tend to find him arty-farty.
Chunks of Italian text, taken from Dante;
a line of Sanskrit (Shanti, Shanti, Shanti);[1]
archaic spelling, Greek, obscure quotes
('The Waste Land' finished up with umpteen notes);
and words you've never come across before
that ought to be prohibited by law –
e.g. polyphiloprogenitive
(there is a clutch of others I could give,
like 'phthisic', 'sutler' and 'unfractuous').
Despite this, the impression made on us
is of a serious questioner exploring.
He may confuse us, but he's never boring;
lines flash like lightning across our eyes,
and we discover, to our great surprise,
that some of them are burnt into our brain!
For many readers, April will remain
the cruellest month, when shoots start coming out

---

1   'The peace which passeth understanding' is Eliot's approximate
translation. It is the last line of 'The Waste Land' (1922).

but find no sustenance, and die from drought —
that's from 'The Waste Land', whose ground-breaking text
shows metaphoric muscles being flexed!
This work, released when he was 33,
has started something of an industry;
with hindsight, no one could dispute the claim
that 'poetry' was never quite the same.
The disillusioned post-war generation,
attracted by his spiritual frustration,
acclaimed him; but he said his mood was due
to crises he himself was passing through,
not to the European cataclysm.
He then embraced Anglo-Catholicism,
and *Four Quartets* suggest less inner doubt –
there's Reason, if his Rhyme can work it out!
Faber & Faber, which was then (as now)
a publisher for those of higher brow,
made him an editor, then a director;
the English-speaking literary sector
moved in the shadow of his presence there
(a plaque now marks the place in Russell Square,
which authors must have gone to with a sense
not of a meeting, but an *audience*).
His feline rhymes, intended for the Young,[2]
were posthumously pantomimed and sung
in *Cats*, Andrew Lloyd Webber's lively staging;
so now 'T. S.' was positively engaging,
an irony compounded by the fact
that his own plays were very rarely packed.[3]
The village of East Coker, Somerset,
which formed the subject of his Second Quartet,

---

2   *Old Possum's Book of Practical Cats*, published in 1939. The musical
    version was first staged in 1981.
3   The best-known of Eliot's verse-plays is *Murder in the Cathedral*
    (1935), about the martyrdom of Thomas Becket (q.v.).

received his ashes when he was cremated
(his forbears toiled here, then emigrated);
his First Quartet ('Burnt Norton'), to my mind
contains a telling statement: 'Humankind
Cannot bear very much reality.'
If he was here now, would he still agree?

80.

SIR CHARLES SPENCER 'CHARLIE' CHAPLIN

16 APRIL 1889 – 25 DECEMBER 1977

Film actor and director

His London childhood was grim indeed –
he'd even lived within the Workhouse gate.
But his determination to succeed
made Charlie internationally Great.

He joined Fred Karno's troupe, which sailed west,
performing slapstick in the USA.
Mack Sennett saw his act, and was impressed[1]
(Charlie played 'The Inebriate', by the way).

'I've started Keystone Films. Stay on out here,
give up the stage, and try the screen instead!'
So Charlie did, and in one hectic year
35 movies were distributed!

Most were one-reel films (not very long).
They'd have a vague idea, perhaps a title,
and make the plot up as they went along.
There had to be a chase, though – this was vital!

The outfit Charlie thought he'd like to use
(the skimpy jacket, cane, and bowler hat,
the baggy trousers and the outsize shoes)
became his famous trademark. After that

---

1   Mack Sennett, American film producer (1880–1960)

he made more films for other companies –
another 35 in fact, all told.
Then, with two other actor friends of his,[2]
he formed a studio that they controlled –

United Artists, which employed them too!
And now he hit his own creative heights
with *Limelight*, *Modern Times*, *Monsieur Verdoux*,
The Gold Rush and *The Circus*, *City Lights*

(his final silent film); and famously
his Hitler send-up in *The Great Dictator* –
a satire on Nazi Germany,
released in 1940. Two years later,

he made a bad mistake by going round
praising the Russians for their brave resistance.
In 1952, when London-bound,
he learned that at the FBI's insistence

he wouldn't be permitted to return –
he was a Communist, or so they said.
To minimise the tax on what he'd earn,
the Chaplins moved to Switzerland instead.

Ensconced within his mountainous stockade,
he planned more films (completing only two),[3]
wrote scores for many of the ones he'd made,
and raised more children. He had quite a few!

---

2   With Mary Pickford (1893–1979) and Douglas Fairbanks
     (1883–1939), he founded United Artists in 1919.
3   Neither very successful: *A King in New York* (1957) and *A Countess
     from Hong Kong* (1967).

Two by his first wife, eight by No. 4 –
his much-beloved and level-headed Oona.[4]
It would have saved a lot of stress before,
if he had met a soulmate like her sooner.

The capitalist system, Charlie stated,
was unfair, and already in decay.
But being rich need not be deprecated –
'I'm one of those who will be swept away!'

Belief brought little comfort, in his view.
He asked: 'Why should this life be such a trial
that people stand for ages in a queue,
hoping that I will briefly make them smile?'

---

4 His fourth wife Oona (1926–1991) was the daughter of the
playwright Eugene O'Neill. They were married in 1943.

81

DAME AGATHA MARY CLARISSA CHRISTIE

15 SEPTEMBER 1890 – 12 JANUARY 1976

The world's best-selling mystery writer

Agatha Mary Clarissa Miller
first thought of tackling a thriller
when still a child in Torquay –
the youngest of a brood of three
whose father (from the USA)
earned quite enough for them to pay
an ample staff, which meant they passed
as being truly Middle Class.
She taught herself to write and read
(skills any author's bound to need),
for she was never sent to school.
Young wives-to-be were, as a rule,
despatched to continental places
to learn the necessary graces;
she went to Paris for a spell,
and must have done extremely well,
for several hectic years ensued
while she was amorously pursued.
Though Major Lucy thought he'd won,
no race is over till it's run –
Lieutenant Christie came along...
With her fiancé in Hong Kong,
what was poor Agatha to do?
Her writing name provides a clue!

The War began; he got some leave
and married her on Christmas Eve,
1914. With him away
she started nursing in Torbay,
and later learned how to dispense,
mixing the raw ingredients,
which later proved a wise decision –
her villains poison with precision!
To pass the time till he returned,
she used the chemistry she'd learned
to draft a convoluted plot –
and Hercule Poirot was begot.
He triumphed, using (as he said)
the grey cells in his egg-shaped head.[1]
Two publishers rejected it;
but after pondering a bit
(two years since getting the MS),
the third she sent it to said 'Yes!'.

More manuscripts were soon despatched.
Ten years after Hercule was hatched,
sharp-eyed Jane Marple joined the force![2]
Agatha went through a divorce,
but took the plunge a second time
the year Miss Marple turned to crime...
She'd gone off to Baghdad, and spent
some happy days inside a tent
(the on-site team invited her
to help them excavate at Ur),
meeting young Max Mallowan there
and marrying him. She learned to share
his interest in ancient places,
and used them for some Poirot cases.

---

1   *The Mysterious Affair at Styles*, 1920
2   *The Murder at the Vicarage*, 1930.

Ninety-eight books and 15 plays!
The Mousetrap ceases to amaze
now half a century's gone by –
it's part of London, like the Eye.
What Agatha has left behind
is still assiduously mined.
Billions of sales, endless TV...
and all this started in Torquay!

82

AMY JOHNSON
1 JULY 1903 – 5 JANUARY 1941

The first woman to fly solo from England to Australia

...Here's the difficult bit...

My imagination boggles,
gazing at the fragile thing;[1]
Amy puts on cap and goggles,
Jason (that's its name) takes wing!
Hardly heavier than air,
open cockpit lashed with rain;
land each night, no matter where –
40 winks, and off again...

---

1   Her aeroplane was acquired by the Science Museum,
      London in 1931.

Amy, having learned to fly,
set out in determined mood.
'Reach Australia or die'
seemed to be her attitude.
Bare necessities aboard –
compass, air-speed, tilt and height.
Up into the sky she roared,
out of touch and out of sight!

Twenty days of constant tension,[2]
facing problems on her own
(Hull to London, I should mention,
was the farthest she had flown).
Upward of a million waited
when she flew back home at last.
King George had her decorated;
honours followed thick and fast...

Found her status hard to bear –
shining star of every show!
Broke more records in the air
(Cape Town twice, plus Tokyo).
Gave the married state a try –
lasted three years, sad to say.
Still, they were the first to fly
from England to the USA.[3]

---

2   Amy landed in Darwin on 24 May 1930 after leaving Croydon on
the fifth.

3   She married the pilot James Mollison (1905–1959). Their 1933
transatlantic flight took 39 hours.

War began, and she applied
to fly new aircraft to their bases –
hardly had the paintwork dried
than they were wanted by the Aces.
One dark day, her bright machine
hit the Thames, and Amy drowned.
Even though her plunge was seen,
her airy frame was never found...

83.

LAURENCE KERR, LORD OLIVIER

22 MAY 1907 – 11 JULY 1989

Our most famous Shakespearean actor

If you were casting for a play
it helped to have Olivier,
although he wasn't reckoned Great
until, when he was 28,
he took part at the New Theatre
with Gielgud (then known the better)[1]
in *Romeo and Juliet*.
This triumph was a major factor
in launching Larry as an actor –
the plays that Shakespeare wrote (q.v.)
remained his speciality!

In that year (1935)
there also happened to arrive
another incandescent star
who tripped the boards not very far
from these engaging gentlemen –
Leigh Holman's young wife Vivien.[2]
Miss Leigh, as she was known on stage,
was praised on each theatre page
for putting everything she'd got
into the devil of a plot –
to serve a scheming rival's ends,

---

1   John Gielgud (1904–2000)
2   Vivien Leigh (1913–1967)

a woman of the streets pretends
a chasteness she does not possess,
and gets a Marquis in a mess.
The Mask of Virtue was its title,
and her convincingness was vital.
Film-maker Alexander Korda
decided he could just afford her,
and signed her, with Olivier.
The two had clicked (as people say)
before the film was in the can;[3]
but Larry was a married man...

The life these lovers came to lead
was destined to be fraught indeed,
though while they blossomed, he and she
were reverenced like Royalty.
But let's get back to stage and screen.
The only way he can be seen
is in his films, from which he made
far more than the theatre paid;
but, as he openly confessed,
the playhouse suited him the best,
allowing him to live the part
without the need to stop and start.
The fifties saw a change of mood;
a painful period ensued
with Vivien now high, now low,
a person whom he didn't know –
when manic, nothing could contain her.
John Osborne's hit *The Entertainer*,
portraying Britain in decay,
exemplified the post-war play:
Larry, momentously, was cast
as somebody whose time is past –

---

3   *Fire over England*, 1937

a comic no one wants to see!
Joan Plowright, his new wife-to-be,
was in it too, so things got better.
He led the National Theatre
during its opening decade
(which wasn't happy, I'm afraid),
became ennobled as a peer,
and then (a curtain call) filmed *Lear*...
But when we think of him today
it's in the film of Shakespeare's play
Henry V, before the breach,
delivering the famous speech
that galvanised his happy few
to show what desperate Brits could do![4]

---

[4] Olivier also directed this film, which was made in 1944.

84

ALISTAIR COOKE

20 NOVEMBER 1908 – 30 MARCH 2004

Who broadcast a weekly 'Letter from America'

Alfred (Alistair) Cooke
is a Brit in my book
though some readers may think
he shattered the link
when he crossed the Atlantic.
Let's not be pedantic –
UK born, UK bred,
it can hardly be said
that he changed in essentials
with his altered credentials.
In fact, his success
lay in being much less
a Yank than a Brit,
and this made him a Hit –
his weekly transmission
(with no intermission)
lasted 58 years.
Although to our ears
his voice was accented,
our man represented
true Britishness there –
they thought Alistair
all the things we should be,
quintessentially!
When at Cambridge, in fact,
he'd been tempted to act
(which is why he arranged
for his name to be changed),

and he tinkled the keys
with consummate ease;
but to Yale he went,
and the two years he spent
made him keen to remain.
Still, he came back again
to begin his career
with the Beeb over here
in late '34,
which was not long before
a rich divorcee
made King Edward-to-be
decide to stand down
and let Love win the crown.[1]
Across the Atlantic
the public were frantic
to know what was what;
as the man on the spot,
the States were enabled
(from the stories he cabled)
to keep up with the drama,
and once things had grown calmer,
the fee he was paid
meant he went back, and stayed!
With the war lost and won,
the Beeb had begun
a 13-week trial –
each week he'd compile
a Letter designed
with the British in mind
in which he'd report
on whatever he thought
might be apt, or amuse.
He knew what to choose,

---

1   Edward VIII renounced his title to marry Wallis Simpson in
     December 1936.

for his Letters extended
till the century ended!
When the time came to write
his final 'Goodnight',
death was five weeks away.[2]
There are some who would say
that his whimsical sense
of the course of events
leaves us short of a clue
to his own point of view;
but standing apart
was a part of his art,
like the English he'd write –
itself a delight.
'Fantastic' is not
encountered a lot,
or 'amazing', or 'great',
which journalists state
as a matter of course,
so they've lost all their force;
attend, and you'll hear
semi-colons appear
in those finely-judged pauses
dividing his clauses!
One story he missed
had a personal twist –
the secret removal
(without his approval)
of the bones he possessed,
so they buried the rest.
But by then, as we say,
he had called it a day...

---

2   The first letter was broadcast on 24 March 1946, the last on
        20 February 2004.

85

ALAN MATHISON TURING

23 JUNE 1912 – 7 JUNE 1954

Mathematician and computer pioneer

A mop of hair, a boyish grin,
the thirties Cambridge scene...
What field is he working in?
What does this long word mean?

The *Entscheidungsproblem*, you see,
is what made Alan Great.
Although it's Double Dutch to me,
it helped him contemplate

an automatic calculator
that could, as we'd say now,
be *programmed* by an operator –
but no one then knew how!

Though his Machine was of the mind,
its obvious potential
for cracking codes of every kind
made real ones essential

when war began. The tangled Morse
the enemy was using
could not be read, and this, of course,
made matters more confusing.

So his brainchild was created.
It made a fearful din,

giving off sparks as wheels rotated
once data was fed in.

Though others also shared the load,
his concept was the key.
The cracking of Enigma's code
needs no more words from me.

This was his happiest time, it's thought,
decoding in Hut 8[1]
at Bletchley Park. The battle fought,
disaster lay in wait...

A homosexual act was then
a culpable offence.
A blackmailer knew who and when;
Alan had no defence.

To meet the measure of his crime
there were two options. (a)
hormonal treatment for a time,
or (b) be locked away.[2]

Barred from the work he had been doing,
by his own hand he died.
They found an apple he'd been chewing,
containing cyanide...

The secret cloak he had to wear
prevented recognition.
So at the keyboard, say a prayer
for this great mathematician!

---

1   Hut 8 was where the German naval signals were decrypted.
2   He chose a year's course of oestrogen injections, with unpleasant
        side effects such as breast development.

86

SIR FREDERICK HOYLE
24 JUNE 1915 – 20 AUGUST 2001

Who showed that we are made of stardust

Yorkshire born and Yorkshire bred,
there was no suppressing Fred.
He may have lost the Nobel Prize
for daring to hypothesise
that space-borne viruses could be
the evolutionary key
to wiping out the weaker sort;
he thought our timescale much too short
for evolution of the kind
that Darwin (q.v.) had in mind.

Still, Fred's undoubted expertise
lay less in matters such as these
than in the physics of Creation...
Based on the well-known observation
that galaxies are in recession,
the cosmological profession
accepted that this had to mean
the Biggest Bang you'd ever seen
had started everything in motion.
Fred thought this a preposterous notion![1]
His new idea, the Steady State,
appeared in 1948,
when he (with Gold, and Bondi too)[2]

---

1   Ironically, it was Fred who coined the contemptuous term
       'Big Bang'.
2   Thomas Gold (1920–2004), Hermann Bondi (1919–2005)

challenged the 'all from nothing' view.
New galaxies could be created
to keep space fully populated
through Einstein's Relativity
(according to their formulae),
so there had never been a start!
But then the theory fell apart...
A faint but most insistent hiss
turned out to be the cause of this –
the Big Bang's evanescent trace,
enfeebled now by Time and Space.[3]

Some time before this serious blow
(in fact, just 50 years ago),
Fred managed to make perfect sense
of how the different elements
came into being. It was thought
that hydrogen, the simplest sort,
had been created right away –
but there are 92 today;
and if there weren't, there wouldn't be
an Earth at all, or you (or me)!
With William Fowler, Fred computed[4]
how elements could be transmuted
inside a star that gets too hot
(carbon, zinc, oxygen, the lot) –
and once its heady days are over
it blows up as a *supernova*.
Let aeons pass, and then, perhaps,
its scattered atoms will collapse
to form a planet, which may be
home for the likes of you (or me)!

---

3   This 'background radiation' was discovered in the mid-1960s.
4   William Alfred Fowler (1911–1995), but not Fred, won the
     Nobel Prize for Physics in 1983.

Before Sir Patrick's *Sky At Night*,
Fred's broadcasts, and the books he'd write,
gave him unchallenged pride of place
regarding things to do with Space;
moreover, his prodigious pen
wrote science fiction now and then.
The Black Cloud is perhaps the best –
a cloud of matter comes to rest
around the Sun! This gripping book
is out of print, but have a look
and see what Amazon can do
(when I last looked, they listed two).

87, AND 88,

FRANCIS HARRY COMPTON CRICK

8 JUNE 1916 – 28 JULY 2004

AND

ROSALIND ELSIE FRANKLIN

25 JULY 1920 – 16 APRIL 1958

Who investigated the nature of the DNA molecule

It may seem a bit thick
that Watson and Crick
did not include Rosalind's name
as a co-author too,
for it's certainly true
that her own research bolstered their claim

to have DNA sussed!
Her role's still discussed
in the kudos the other two earned,
for her patient endeavour
won no credit whatever
as far as the public's concerned!

Ironically,
a physics degree
began the career of Crick.
So he didn't start gaining
information pertaining
to what makes all living things tick

until after the War,
when Sir Lawrence Bragg saw[1]
that Crick might decode DNA,
and help Cambridge to win
the race they were in
with Pauling & Co. (USA).[2]

The score was 0–1,
for what Pauling had done
was to work out how *proteins* are made.
But DNA might
(if the Light Blues were right)
be the site of the gene that displayed

the code for a lark,
and the code for a shark,
and the code for a feather or fin;
and within our own Genus
the difference between us,
such as colour of eyes, hair or skin.

Crick worked tirelessly
with a young PhD
from Chicago, James Watson. The pair[3]
thought that X-rays might show
what they needed to know;
but their photographs didn't compare

with Rosalind's own
(some of which they were shown).
So although they conceived DNA
as two corkscrews aligned,
with their turns intertwined,
Ms Franklin informed them: 'No way!

---

1   William Lawrence Bragg (1890–1971).
2   Linus Carl Pauling (1901–1994), legendary American chemist.
3   James Dewey Watson (b. 1928).

'The parts on the outside
have got to be inside –
it'll need to be tweaked a bit more!'
They saw she was right;
and more clues came to light
in an X-ray they found in her drawer

showing DNA twisting
(the best yet existing).
This helped them, of that there's no doubt.
But there was, even so,
a long way to go,
before they had worked it all out!

So the Nobel Prize could
have been hers (as it should),
but the medals were chosen too late,[4]
for they'd laid her to rest.
Still, her DNA test
would undoubtedly show she was Great!

---

4   For their work on DNA, Crick, Watson and a third researcher named
Maurice Wilkins were awarded the Nobel Prize in 1962.

89.

GEOFFREY LEONARD, LORD CHESHIRE

7 SEPTEMBER 1917 – 31 JULY 1992

World War Two pilot and charity founder

More than a hundred times, he flies
into the searchlights and the flak.
His going causes no surprise;
the marvel is his coming back.

At 30 outings, I believe,
the grim returns begin to show
good betting odds that he'll receive
an invitation from below.

Was it because he didn't care
that he defied the statistician?
Or was he wafted through the air
to save him for his post-war mission?

Leonard came down to earth at last...
The fight was won; what could he do?
The fellowship of War was past –
a lonely Peace brought something new.

In his vast empty house, Le Court
(in Hampshire), he set out to try
communal living, of the sort
that had sustained him in the sky.

A RHYMING HISTORY

It didn't work – the group dispersed,
but one, with cancer, asked to stay,
and Leonard had to have him nursed...
His second life was under way!

Le Court filled up, so other places
(the first in Cornwall and in Kent)
were found, to help these desperate cases
face up to their predicament.

Some star had set him on his course
to be a Charitable Provider;
he met another driving force
and she became his wife – Sue Ryder.[1]

Then Leonard lost a lung; but still
he found he had sufficient puff
to spearhead their campaigns, until
his flesh, not spirit, said 'Enough!'

His Charity, so I have read,
thinks 'Cheshire' rings no bells today.
One title they've put up instead
is 'Equability UK'.

---

1   Sue Ryder (1923-2000), founder of the well-known charity.

90.

DONALD CAMPBELL
23 MARCH 1921 – 4 JANUARY 1967

Who died attempting the water-speed record

When Donald Campbell's *Bluebird* crashed,
it was a quirk of fate.
His record-breaking hopes were smashed,
and that's what made him Great.[1]

---

1   Donald Campbell was listed eighty-ninth in the BBC's 2002 poll of
     Top Britons. His father, Malcolm Campbell (1885–1948) broke the
     water-speed record four times between 1 September 1937 and
     19 August 1939, but was not nominated as a BBC Great.

91, AND 92,

JOHN WINSTON ONO LENNON
9 OCTOBER 1940 – 8 DECEMBER 1980
AND
SIR JAMES PAUL MCCARTNEY
B, 18 JUNE 1942

Songwriters for the Beatles

Now we're much older, grey in our hair,
since the world was young,
hear our grown-up children saying, wish we'd been
London swingers, part of the scene.
Mother and Father having a ball
40 years before!
Do you still kiss her,
would you still miss her,
now you're 64?

Turntables spun them through our decade,
far as Abbey Road.
Sounded like the sixties were the time to be!
What did it feel like, suddenly free?
Pop pirates challenged Radio Lux,
skirts rose more and more.
How could you tell then
how far to go then
back in '64?

Lennon–McCartney on 78s,
drinking Hirondelle.[1]
Fingers creeping up her thigh, it's quite OK,
just heard there's a Pill on the way.
Wait on the pavement while she goes in,
never late before.
Either miscarried
or had to get married,
back in '64.

World just emerging from the shadow of death.
When we went to bed
weren't all that convinced there'd be another day,
Jack confronting Mr K.![2]
London a target, Swinging or not,
in this final war.
Lap of the gods,
what are the odds
I'll reach 64?

Beatles and Dylan, Carnaby Street,
New Wave, *Private Eye*,
Supermac, Profumo scandal, Labour in,[3]
Ban the Bomb, and England win!
Lennon–McCartney made a noise
never heard before.
Sixties were teeming,
sixties were screaming,
sixties were the Fabulous Four!

---

1   Trendy plonk from Tesco, three for £1 (I think).
2   The Cuba Crisis, October 1962, when President Kennedy demanded that Mr Khrushchev remove Soviet missiles.
3   The Profumo Affair rocked Macmillan's government in June 1963.

93

STEPHEN WILLIAM HAWKING
B. 8 JANUARY 1942

Theoretical physicist

When talking
Of Hawking
My conceptual ceiling
Is suddenly feeling
Low.

His tutors had never met
Such a laid-back undergraduate.
He didn't seem to try.
His mind was sky-high.
(That's why.)

Would the fame he's enjoyed
Have been the same if his body had not been destroyed
By progressive motor-neurone disease,
Which has gradually made his muscles freeze?
Perhaps not.
But the brain that he has got
Would have taken him far,
Although he almost certainly would not have evolved into such
a superstar.

The trouble for me is
I find it hard to understand his discoveries...

For example, he knows
Where material that has been blasted out from a dying star or has
otherwise found itself near the event horizon of an exceedingly
dense object, goes
When it vanishes from sight
Inside a Hole that gives out no light.

And he hopes to find out
what happened 0.0000000000000000000000000000000000000000
0001 of a second (about)[1]
After God said 'Let's go!'
Although
He does share the hunch
That the Universe really happened by chance, when the forces of
expansion (the Big Bang) and contraction (gravity) just happened
to balance so closely that it didn't either collapse straight away or
explode so fast that stars didn't have time to form, thus giving rise
to the pleasing concept of the Universe being a 'free lunch';
i.e.
there would have been no need for a Divinity.

Um.

In 1962
He knew
That in three years he would be dead.
(So they said.)
Now almost the only thing that is there
Of the Man in the Chair
Is his Will.
He is almost completely still.
All he can move is his eye.
By controlling his eye movements he can stimulate a voice
synthesiser, on which he has had to rely

---

1   10^{-43} second (known as the Planck epoch).

Since 1985.
How much longer can this Great Brit survive?
What will he think
When he can no longer
blink?

94

DAME ANITA PERELLA RODDICK

B. 23 OCTOBER 1942

Who started The Body Shop, and campaigns against commercial and political abuses

Brave Littlehampton! Thanks to you
the sunny Sussex coast
produced, in 1942,
a Great of whom to boast.

A RHYMING HISTORY

Her mother was a restaurateur.
Anita fetched and carried,
travelled the world (which sobered her),
came home again, and married

a man named Gordon Roddick, who
decided in due course
that what he simply had to do
was ride upon a horse

from Buenos Aires all the way
to New York! Off he went.
Anita had to make things pay,
and found a shop to rent.

The scents and lotions purchased here
(made to her recipe)
meant buyers' consciences were clear
environmentally!

No animals had been degraded;
moreover, she refused
to buy from anyone who traded
where workers were abused.

Containers were recycled too,
to everyone's surprise
(though she's confessed that this was due
to problems with supplies).

Her Body Shop had found a niche,
and Gordon had his ride.
In ten years they were pretty rich;
in 30, she'd decide

to give the lowest of the low
that suffer on this planet
the 50 million quid or so
she'd earned since she began it.

She's now reacted to a test
for Hepatitis C.
'It's shattering,' she has confessed,
'but that's not stopping me!'

95.

SIR RICHARD CHARLES NICHOLAS BRANSON

B. 18 JULY 1950

Financial empire-builder and adventurer

Sir Richard Branson, famed entrepreneur,
was found to suffer from dyslexia
long after he had given up at school –
that's why they thought him something of a fool.
To compensate for problems with his spelling
he set himself to learn the art of selling –
among his wares were home-grown Christmas trees.
Failing to make much profit out of these,
he turned to flogging records much more cheaply
than High Street shops like Smith's, which hurt them deeply.
This venture introduced the Virgin label,
and in due course our buccaneer was able
to launch the Virgin Record Company!
His empire grew exponentially –
Virgin Atlantic (1984)
entered a David and Goliath war
with giant British Airways, which he won.
As well as work, he had a lot of fun
spending some of the millions in the bank
on transatlantic runs. His speedboat sank
in '85, the finishing line in sight;
in '86, though, everything went right,
beating the clock in *Challenger II*.[1]

---

1   New York to the Scillies in 3 days 8.5 hours

In '87, another record beckoned...
He waited till the winds were opportune
and crossed again – in a hot-air balloon,
the first time anyone had made the trip!
This mode of travel had him in its grip –
in '98, his *Virgin Global Flyer*
(with all the propane that it would require)
made an attempted circumnavigation,
but to his understandable frustration
he had to land when halfway round or so –
which some might think quite far enough to go.[2]
As yet, he hasn't launched a company
that flies balloons to get from A to B;
but he does plan, with everything so Green,
to sell the cleanest fuel we've yet seen.
So Richard Branson really is unique!
Because of this, I hesitate to speak
about his Virgin Trains; I'll simply say
that some of them are subject to delay.

---

2   From Morocco to Hawaii

96

SIR TIMOTHY JOHN BERNERS-LEE

B. 8 JUNE 1955

Inventor of the World Wide Web

Sir Tim Berners-Lee
thought of http://,[1]
hence the Web that we use every day.
It's a great idea, which
could have made him quite rich,
but instead he just gave it away!

---

1   Hypertext Transfer Protocol.

His numeracy
helped with http://,
and his debt to his parents was great.[2]
Squares, cosines and means
were a part of his genes,
and they talked about Maths when they ate.

For two decades, maybe,
before http://,
the Internet's links were evolving.
It didn't do much,
just kept people in touch –
so here was a problem worth solving...

For Sir Tim could now see
that with http://
it could offer whole *pages* to read!
With unparalleled fervour
he constructed a Server,
since that was the gadget he'd need.

Eventually,
using http://,
he launched (on 6/8/91)
his brilliant creation.
What hyper-elation –
the world-weaving Web had begun!

Sir Tim gave it free
(even http://),
for the good of the globe as a whole.
A personal site
should be everyone's right –
and that is his ultimate goal!

---

2   His parents belonged to the team developing the very early
       Manchester University Mark I computer.

A RHYMING HISTORY

The expediency
with which http://
facilitates criminal links
is greatly outweighed
by the friends it has made,
or at least so Sir Timothy thinks.

Realistically
we've *got* http:// –
it was bound to come sooner or later...
So let's honour Sir Tim,
for we owe it to him
that the world has grown smaller (or greater?)!

97.

DIANA, PRINCESS OF WALES

1 JULY 1961 – 31 AUGUST 1997

'The People's Princess'

What were you doing when you heard
the fatal car crash had occurred?
Perhaps a friend rang up, and said
'Did you know Princess Di is dead?'
Or maybe you switched on, to see
what sort of weather it would be,
and lamentation far and near
poured down from the ionosphere?
A woman we had never seen
except as someone on a screen
confronted by a storm of light
that flashed on her Olympian height
left us bereft, as loved ones do;
she seemed like somebody we knew,
playing the princess for a time
during that sell-out pantomime
until the horses turned to mice,
and in the end she paid the price.
That was the heart of her appeal –
she wasn't royal, she was real!
The kingdom mourned, and strangers cried,
because a part of them had died.

98.

SIR STEPHEN GEOFFREY REDGRAVE

B. 23 MARCH 1962

Our golden Olympian

Sir Stephen Redgrave pulled an oar
better than anyone before.
He won (if I may put it so)
at five Olympics in a row,[1]
plus nine world-class events elsewhere,
more weight of gold than he can wear;

---

1   Between 1984 and 2000.

and it is only fair to note
that Matthew Pinsent helped his boat
eleven times to row to gold.[2]
At 38, he'd grown too old
to keep the younger ones behind,
and so he honourably resigned;
but having shipped his golden oars
he champions a worthy cause
entitled The Steve Redgrave Trust,
where new suggestions are discussed
for helping youngsters to succeed
(especially those in need).
His Leisurewear concern (5G)
went fair trade very recently;
and you can hire him for Dinners,
to show how we can all be winners.

---

2   Sir Matthew Clive Pinsent (b. 1970) also holds 14 Olympic and
     world-class gold medals.

JOANNE 'J. K.' ROWLING

B. 31 JULY 1965

Author of the record-breaking Harry Potter *books*

Jo Rowling's done it very well,
as far as I can see.
She's written books that sell like hell
and kept her privacy.

She studied French at Exeter,
where I was working too.
Did I, perhaps, bump into her?
Did I say 'After you'?

She started there in '83
(according to her site),
and having taken her degree
she 'temped', and tried to write.

It may have been a Virgin Train
(owned by another Great)[1]
that put the Boy into her brain
during an endless wait...

'He simply fell into my head'
before it moved again.
But famously, as she has said,
she didn't have a pen!

---

1   See entry for Sir Richard Branson.

She rushed home teeming, found a jotter,
and scribbled her idea.
That was the start of Harry Potter;
but later in the year

her mother died (she had MS)
when she was in her prime.
Nor was Jo's marriage a success.
She had a testing time.

A baby daughter (Jessica);
an Edinburgh flat;
to write, though, she would much prefer
a café, where she sat

with Jessica (and Harry too)
and coffee in her cup.
Four years after he'd told her to,
she typed his story up.

A hopeful agent said 'OK',
but publishers were cool.
They didn't like her protégé
or Hogwarts Wizard School.

A whole frustrating year went by
till Bloomsbury agreed
the story might be worth a try –
success *not* guaranteed!

But readers loved the wizardry.
The Stone had started Rowling.[2]
Her book began an industry
she's had a job controlling.

---

2   *Harry Potter and the Philosopher's Stone*, the first of the series, was
       published in June 1997 in the UK, October 1998 in the USA.

Jo's now a dollar billionaire.
No books are snapped up faster.
Still, as I'm sure she is aware,
success could have by-passed her.

How often was her first book read
and sent back with a 'No'?
How long before her agent said:
'I've found no takers, Jo'?

Was this when Harry Potter saw
he had some more to do?
He'd stopped her train five years before –
he'd get her published, too!

100.

DAVID BECKHAM

B. 2 MAY 1975

England footballer and celebrity

Keep kicking a ball
against a brick wall,
and there's no knowing what may occur.
You might hear a shout
to get the hell out –
or you could end up marrying *Her*.

He was one of a group
who joined Ferguson's troupe[1]
as part of a Youth Training Scheme.
His folks were delighted –
Manchester United!
They'd shout for their favourite team,

though they tended to play
a long way away
from Leytonstone, London E10!
At the age of 19
their offspring was seen
in the red shirt. What happened since then

the entire world knows.
He hit highs, he hit lows;
depending on how the ball bent,
its subliminal flight
might go left, might go right –
Beckham's free kicks became an event!

---

1   Sir Alex Ferguson (b. 1941) has been the manager of Manchester
United since 1986.

But how deep was the trough
after being sent off
when the England team faced Argentina![2]
He became, for a spell,
our Player from Hell,
so we have to applaud his demeanour

for so bravely pursuing
through the jeers and the booing
(which must have been pretty unnerving),
his unstoppable aim
to get back in the game –
which, unlike his free kicks, was unswerving!

And get back he did.
The Leytonstone Kid
was redeemed in the Year of the Dome.
He captained the side,
and with Posh as his bride
they set up a well-publicised home.[3]

The crowds that had roared
at the goals he had scored
now applauded a greater event.
The Posh–Beckham team
was a marketer's dream
(e.g. aftershave, spectacles, scent...)!

Though he's gone off to play
for a team in LA,
he intends bending balls left and right
if England should need
his help to succeed –
and I have a strong feeling they might!

---

2   Beckham was sent off for a retaliatory foul during the match on
     30 June 1998.
3   Victoria Caroline Adams (b. 1975), one of the Spice Girls
     (1994–2000). They were married on 4 July 1999.

INDEX

Brit Wit

The perfect riposte for every social occasion

Edited by
Susie Jones

BRIT WIT
The perfect riposte for every social occasion

Edited by Susie Jones

£8.99

H/B

ISBN 13: 978 1 84024 415 1

Ever been at a loss for words? Ever wished that the perfect wry remark (or putdown) would spring to mind? The great, the good, the intellectual and the downright insulting can all be found in *Brit Wit*.

Densely populated with wonderful one-liners from such formidable figures as Churchill and Shakespeare to the more recent luminaries of British stage, screen and society, *Brit Wit* celebrates all that makes Britain brilliant.

'*If you prefer your humour condensed into one-liners try* Brit Wit, *a beautifully presented catalogue of jests, asides, ripostes and insults*'   Daily Mail

'*Plumped with zippy one-liners and comebacks for any occasion, this book collects the best zingers from the greatest minds in British history. Old Blighty sparkles in this clever compendium of witty, wordy gems*'
Andrew Young, The Good Book Guide

'Brit Wit *celebrates all that makes Britain brilliant*!'
Motoring and Leisure magazine

Old Git Wit

Wit

Quips and quotes for the young at heart

OLD GIT WIT
Quips and Quotes for the Young at Heart

Richard Benson

£8.99

H/B

ISBN 13: 978 1 84024 542 4

You've made it. Old age. You want to make the most of your golden years and are finding yourself stereotyped and sidelined. But you're not the doddering geriatric people think you are.

'Get inspired by this collection of senior sagacity and elderly erudition and show those young whippersnappers that old is the new young. If you are turning into an old git get this and put a smile on your face' The Shetland Times

Made in BRITAIN

The Best of Quintessentially British Companies

JAMES FIELDING

MADE IN BRITAIN
The Best of Quintessentially British Companies

James Fielding

£9.99

H/B

ISBN 13: 978 1 84024 605 6

Like beans on toast, big red buses and cups of tea, there are some things that are just plain British. But with global brands on the up and up, is it still possible to buy British?

Which consumer products are still made in the UK? *Made in Britain* gives potted histories and fascinating photographs from days gone by of businesses such as:

- Gieves and Hawkes, who equipped Livingstone and Stanley for their central Africa expeditions
- Hiatt, suppliers of handcuffs to police forces around the world
- Jaques, who brought us Snakes and Ladders as well as croquet sets

Some companies are household names, while others are newer or more unusual, but all their standards are exceptionally high. For the nostalgic, the patriotic and those who want to reduce their carbon footprint, this fascinating book will delight and surprise.

www.summersdale.com